I've Got Your Number!

by Doris Webster
and Mary A. Hopkins

NEWCASTLE PUBLISHING CO., INC.
NORTH HOLLYWOOD, CALIFORNIA

Originally published in 1927 by The Century Co.

ISBN: 0-87877-238-3
A Newcastle Classic
First printing 1996
10 9 8 7 6 5 4 3 2 1
Printed in the United States of America.

Cover design © 1996 Michele Lanci-Altomare

I've Got Your Number!
First Series

I'VE GOT YOUR NUMBER

YOUR response to these questions gives the key to your character.

DIRECTIONS (READ CAREFULLY)

Read each of the following questions carefully and after impartial consideration answer each one "yes" or "no."

Do not omit any answer, as omission is construed as a negative answer.

If you feel that you cannot answer definitely "yes" or "no," remember that the situation described should be considered in its usual aspect, without addition of extraordinary circumstances. For example, if the question is, "Would you walk five blocks to see a parade?" do not assume, on the one hand, that you might have sprained your ankle, nor, on the other, that the president of the United States might be marching in the parade.

Answer as fairly as you can what would be your normal reaction under normal conditions.

If you still feel that your answer cannot be a positive "yes" or "no," give whichever answer seems to have the balance of weight on its side. In such questions as, "Do people come to you for advice?" compare yourself with the *average* man or woman, to the best of your ability, and answer accordingly.

To find your key:

Each of the questions in the five groups, including five questions each, must be answered. If your answer is "yes" to three or more of the questions under Group 1, your key number begins with the digit "1." If it is "no," omit "1" from your key number. In the same way, if you answer most of the questions in Group 2 in the affirmative, the number "2" is a digit in your key number; if most of these questions are answered in the negative, "2" is omitted, and so on with each group.

For example, suppose you answer "yes" to the majority of the questions in Group 2, Group 4, and Group 5, and "no" to the majority in Groups 1 and 3, your key number will be 245.

To take other examples, if you answer "yes" to the majority of questions in every group, your key number will be 12345; if "no," it will be 0. If you answer "no" to the majority of questions in each of the first four groups and "yes" to the majority in the last group, your key number will be 5.

When you have ascertained your key number, look it up on page 16 if you are a man or 94 if you are a woman, and you will find your analysis.

EXAMPLE

Group 1		Group 2		Group 3		Group 4		Group 5	
A	Yes	A	No	A	Yes	A	Yes	A	Yes
B	No	B	Yes	B	Yes	B	Yes	B	Yes
C	No	C	Yes	C	No	C	Yes	C	No
D	No	D	Yes	D	No	D	Yes	D	Yes
E	Yes	E	No	E	No	E	Yes	E	No
	No		Yes		No		Yes		Yes
	—		2		—		4		5

Key number = 245

QUESTIONS FOR MEN

For directions see page 1

GROUP I

A—Do you wake up despondent?

B—Do most of the people on the street look dissatisfied?

C—Have you been unlucky in your business relations?

D—Can you hold a grievance three years?

E—Do you think people talk against you behind your back?

GROUP 2

A—Do you prefer to make decisions rather than to let circumstances decide for you?

B—Is success usually the result of honest effort?

C—Do people come to you for advice?

D—Are your mistakes your own fault?

E—Do you get your own way?

GROUP 3

A—Have you definitely planned your career five years ahead?

B—Did you choose your profession or business yourself?

C—Would you accept promotion if it meant much increased work or responsibility?

D—Is a husband's primary duty to be a good provider?

E—Would you rather start your own business than invest in an established enterprise?

GROUP 4

A—Are your day-dreams impractical?

B—Do you put off till to-morrow what you should do to-day?

C—Do you like to be alone with your thoughts?

D—Do people nag you?

E—Are you a fitful worker?

GROUP 5

A—Do you think the average woman is out for all she can get?

B—Do you think early marriage undesirable?

C—Do women shirk?

D—Would you prefer belonging to a club of men only rather than to a club of men and women?

E—When poverty comes in at the door does love fly out of the window?

KEY NUMBERS FOR MEN

CHARACTER STUDIES FOR MEN

Key Number 0

How easily you adjust yourself to any situation! No one knows better than you how to get along with this world, avoiding all unnecessary difficulties, going about your own business, and having a good time while you do it.

If you really want to hear your faults—which you probably do not, for you have no passion for criticism—it might be mentioned that you rather side-step an embarrassing situation if you can; not that you shirk, for you certainly do your share of the world's work, but you do not always grasp the nettle and pull it up. It would not do, however, for you to try to change yourself in this respect, for in the first place you could not, and in the second place most of the people around you would be sorry to see you any different. And, as a matter of fact, you usually get rid of the nettle somehow even if you do not use extreme measures. You are not at all the kind to suffer in silence.

You are ideal in the home, for you take a great interest in it; and ideal in the office, where your work is excellent and where your tact keeps things running smoothly. Although you are not worldly, you might make a good deal of money. You get along with most women so well that you might make the mistake of choosing a sickly tyrant.

Key Number 1

LIFE to you is pretty much one task after another. Although you keep everlastingly at it, your work never grows less, and you get discouraged because you see no let-up ahead of you. You often tell your wife, or maybe it is your mother or your sweetheart, or even a pleasant strange woman whom you meet on the train by chance, that sometimes you are ready to end it all. You never say this to a man for fear he will laugh at you, but women are always kind to you; that is, almost always. Sometimes they get impatient with you because you do not make the most of yourself.

Try to see your life, past, present, and future, like a picture. The past will be very clear, the present should be definite and concrete, while the future will be necessarily a little vague. Nevertheless the future should show bold outlines, which can be altered if necessary. You should have a fairly well formulated idea of what you are going to do and how you are going to do it. As you go ahead with your work you will change your plans more or less to fit into circumstances. Keep details subordinated to your general scheme, putting your mind on them as they come up one by one.

Your greatest asset is a characteristic which may easily become a hindrance if not held in check. You are prone to be contented. This is excellent when applied to your wife and children and house and cigars. But you must not be content with your own achievements to the extent of ceasing your exertions.

Key Number 2

UNLESS you are still very young, you are on various committees and are having difficulty keeping yourself off of others. You are the kind that people turn to for organizing work, first because you do it well, and second because you are willing to take the time from your own affairs in order to get an organization working. You take satisfaction in seeing that it does work, yet you do not insist on bossing the whole show. You are a good executive, especially when it is a matter of managing something not connected with your own business.

You would make an excellent husband, and you would have sense enough to choose a wife wisely and not be carried away by mere youth and beauty. You are fond of children, extremely fond of your home, and would probably like to garden. You like social life for its friendliness but are rather bored by "high life." It doesn't seem to you worth bothering about. You would rather have a good cook than a good butler. You like camping trips, dogs, the theater, and the sea. You would likely be intrigued by a ship model and would like to make one yourself. While you are not looking for trouble, you do not let people impose on you. The woman who marries you is lucky.

Key Number 3

WOMEN like you, and you like women. You have pleasant little ways of helping with the dishes and lugging heavy chairs which endear a guest to a hostess more than the parlor tricks with banjo and cards. A party always "goes" when you are there. What's more, your own women-folks who see you every day all the year are as fond of you as outsiders are, and that is more than many a man can say. Though they prod you, it is for your own good, as they often tell you. The actual reason that you flare up or gloom when they get after you is because your conscience tells you that they are right and that you shouldn't have—well, we'll say no more, for you get the idea.

Once upon a time there was a man who had all the virtues, and several of the vices also. Now, this isn't you, but maybe you will be interested to hear how he treated his tendency to take one more drink. Or maybe it was his habit of playing poker for high stakes. Or maybe it was his exceeding interest in girls he wasn't really interested in at all. He made up in his mind a picture of what he actually wanted in life: high standing among his fellow-men, a moderate income, a good house, a contented wife, two well brought up children. Every night he went to sleep picturing this desire to himself. Soon he began planning how to get these things. Gradually his attention shifted from his old not wholly satisfactory activities and centered itself on attaining the satisfactions he really wanted. In the end he had everything he had listed, a lot more, and had enjoyed the struggle to make good.

Key Number 4

YOU have worked out your own philosophy of life, and it is an excellent one—for you. But not for most men, for not many have your buoyancy, sense of humor, and ability to get a great deal of satisfaction out of little things. You can get just as much pleasure out of a shack as another man gets out of a palace; probably more.

While in some cases it is better for a man to marry his opposite, you would probably do well to choose some one whose outlook on life is rather like your own. She might well have more energy, but if she yearned too much for Rolls-Royces and pearls your marriage might go on the rocks. That would be a pity, for with the right wife you could be ideally happy.

Your personality is intriguing, and it is hard to do it justice. You are friendly toward the world, just and loving. Children amuse you, and you like to give them little presents. You like to watch young animals play. You probably like to smoke, and you would like to fish except that you have notions that the fish do not enjoy it. You are not interested in shooting. You like yourself, and can amuse yourself with your own fancies.

With the wrong environment your rare nature might be harmed, but fortunately you have the habit of getting away from the wrong environment. You do not fight the things that you don't like, but you leave them alone. If there were more like you, the world might not move so fast, but it would be a happier place.

Key Number 5

You have wonderful ability in making the best of things. Maybe you would be better off if you weren't so pleasant and kind and, might one say, easy-going. Can you not remember many occasions when you got into trouble and got other people into trouble also because you took the easiest way out of a difficult situation?

You do hate a row, and you will do anything to avoid one. Can you not learn that sometimes the best, easiest, and kindest method of dealing with persons who are in the wrong is to blow them up good and hard once and for all? You are the type of man who is likely to be imposed on by others. This sort of man is a temptation to other people because he is so obliging about doing work which they should attend to themselves. Deep in his heart he knows that something is being put over on him, and after a while he becomes resentful. Resentment is a slow-burning anger which never did anybody any good. So the thing for you to do is to carry your own burdens with the bravery you have always shown but not take on extra loads which other people should lug themselves.

All of the energy which has been escaping through doing things which are pleasant but harmful should be turned into driving yourself forward toward the goal which you have chosen. If you have not chosen a goal, turn your attention to that matter immediately.

Key Number 12

YOU have one trait that holds you back—unevenness of temperament. That may be due to your early training, or possibly to ill health, but whatever the cause you should overcome it if possible. Of course, you have no special reason for trying to fight your disquieting moods, for you are not particularly anxious to make a spectacular success, but it seems a pity that your really fine qualities should sometimes be overshadowed by your tendency toward trivial complaints.

When you are feeling your best you are a joy to all about you, actively interested in others, and ready to help with their immediate problems. It is only when you are in one of your "Oh, what's the use!" moods that you are something of a trial.

You are liberal, logical, and willing to concede women their due—a priceless quality. Why do you have periods of ill feeling? It is not exactly because of envy, for in your heart you do not covet your neighbor's chauffeur. You really don't care for money very much, yet you are rather indignant when the other fellow has it, especially if he has inherited it.

It might be a good idea if you studied yourself, formulated a philosophy, and remembered it. You have the strength deliberately to remake yourself if you want to, and you are too fine to let yourself run to seed.

Key Number 13

You wonder more frequently than do most people what life is all about anyhow; where we came from, where we are going, where we are now, and if it is really worth while hanging round to find out. When you were a child this characteristic was called "glumness," but you prefer to think of it as despond-ency; if your wife is a wise woman she will accept the characteristic as "going into the silence" and not fuss about it. Maybe she will be smart enough to say: "He has the artist's temperament! The poor dear really should have been a poet!"

Suddenly up from the depths you rise on wings of hope, and, hurrah, it's a fine old world after all! Life is one grand sweet song in your heart. You become the I-can man. You pick up the tasks that have been dragging and send them spinning along toward their goal. You work in a frenzy of energy, and your co-workers seem slow and lazy. You tell your wife, or will when you get one, about the house she is going to have, and together you look over motor-car advertisements. Thanks to these bursts of energy, you keep your job, and progress, but much more slowly than you would if you could hold a steadier gait. Thanks to these spells of delight in life, your wife still loves you, although you demand a deal of patience.

The curious part of it is that your friends have little knowledge of all this tumultuous inner life of yours, for on the surface you seem very much like the other fellows in your set. In the hidden depths of your soul you are unique.

Key Number 14

YOU would like to sit by the fire, wearing an old smoking-jacket and holding the cat. But you would not necessarily be thinking placid thoughts. You are inclined to be introspective and spend considerable time thinking about yourself. But that does not mean that you are selfish. You would forget to feed yourself before you would forget to feed your dog.

You are the kind who gets along very well with a wife, and you are really much happier than you think you are, especially as you secretly believe that some day you are going to startle the world by achieving a great success.

You are a little inclined to carp at other people's suggestions, just for the pleasure of carping, but you are not really hard to get along with, because you are fundamentally reasonable.

Your kindness is perhaps your most lovable characteristic, and your straightforwardness your most admirable. You detest a "smart Aleck" and other forms of cheapness. If some little thing goes wrong, particularly if it means that your feelings are hurt, it may spoil your whole day and color your philosophy ultramarine; but normally your outlook on life is friendly and your attitude toward others free from cynicism.

Key Number 15

YOU have the delightful quality of enjoying your friends, admiring your possessions, fitting your job, and cherishing your intimates. You do not in your heart consider millions worth the effort Rockefeller and Ford had to make to get their money. Oh, you'd take a hundred thousand with thanks if it were just around the corner, but you would not dig to the depths of the earth for it, nor raise great factories, nor direct the activities of ten thousand men, for the sake of making money. You are a steady, conscientious worker, but not an adventurer.

This lack of longing to make yourself miserable doing what you don't want to do, for the sake of something you may never get, sometimes gives you a guilty feeling. Occasionally you feel out of harmony with this world of go-getters. Other people think you are having a grouch, and you yourself are not quite sure what is the trouble. You wonder if you ought to see a doctor, but just then some extra work comes up or the rain stops or you meet a new girl, and you are comfortable again.

I'VE GOT YOUR NUMBER

Girls, wives, aunts, female cousins, and even your mother are continual disappointments to you. Woman, lovely woman, is not, you find, the ministering angel she has been called. You are polite about it—usually—but you do not really think much of women. Your type is likely to remain unmarried, or if married to find it difficult to make sufficient concessions to insure a happy marriage. You expect too much of women, and unless you learn to take them as they are, they will bring you only disappointment and suffering.

Key Number 23

YOU are impeccable! Your only fault is that you are faultless. You are the kind of man whom parents pick out for a girl to marry—and afterward they are able to say that they were right too. You are really kind, not merely lavish, to women; you keep your temper and stick to your job instead of wasting time in idle complaints; you have a sense of humor and can even laugh at yourself sometimes; you are a good workman, a firm but just business man, and would make an excellent husband and a loving father. Not another one of the men analyzed in these pages has the number of good traits that you have.

You see things in their right relationship and can appreciate the other man's point of view and do not feed your vanity by disparaging others. You are the type that is voted the "most popular man" in school or college.

The best of it is that instead of being smugly pleased with the above analysis you are wondering if there isn't something wrong with you just because there is nothing about you to criticize. Don't worry about that; you're all right. Ask the Chamber of Commerce. Ask the men at the club. Ask the girls. Ask mother—she knows!

Key Number 24

YOU do not have to wait till you are dead to have people speak well of you. Sometimes you are ashamed because you think you do not deserve the affection that is showered upon you and the praises that are chorused behind your back. Don't worry; you have your critics, too, who underestimate you as others overestimate you.

You will never be wholly content with yourself, because you will never reach your goal. The reason for this is somewhat peculiar. As you approach your goal, you are looking forward to one further distant and pass your original one without noticing it. Before you finish one achievement, you are already started on the next, although you always complete what you begin.

If you have employees, they like to work for you, and while you are still young they begin referring to you kindly as "the old man," for you are the sort on whom others instinctively lean and to whom they turn for direction and advice. Your wife is—or will be, if you have not yet married—a fortunate woman and knows it. In fact other women feel she is a bit smug about her husband. The worst criticism brought against you is that you are impractical. The finest that is said of you is that you never let anybody down.

Key Number 25

YOU'VE got to be very careful about choosing your wife! Oh, yes, you can get along with most women, and you think one is as good as another; but that's just the trouble. You think of women collectively. You bunch them all together, and you say somewhat cynically, "They're all alike." Some day you may wake up and find out that they aren't. Do make a special study of them before it is too late, with reference not to the color of their eyes and hair (about which you know plenty already) but to their honesty, courage, and brains and unselfishness and similar essentials.

This point must be emphasized, for otherwise there is little to warn you against. You are a good all-round man, popular with men, willing to do your share of unpleasant work, and delightfully sunny by nature. People probably talk about that nice smile of yours.

You like the theater—if it isn't too highbrow—the movies, tennis, and other sports and fishing. You are interested in politics and would enjoy travel. You ought to have a happy life ahead of you if you will get over that slightly cynical attitude toward women. For when you disparage women you are unconsciously laying up trouble for yourself.

Key Number 34

ONCE there was a man who day-dreamed about a boiling tea-kettle, and as a result we have the steamboat. Other men have made their fancies into poems, novels, paintings, and beautiful buildings. You have this same tendency to wander off into an imaginary world, but you have not yet learned that it may be an element of strength instead of a weakness. Nobody but yourself knows how you long to be a success. In fact you will very likely flatly contradict this statement. That is because you do not yet see your way ahead very clearly.

The next time you have a spare hour and there is no one around to jeer at you, write down on a slip of paper all the things you want to do, the positions you want to hold, and the triumphs you wish to accomplish. Draw a line through those that are obviously impossible. From those that are left choose the one that is dearest to you. From now on concentrate on how you can bring to pass what you most desire.

I'VE GOT YOUR NUMBER

Your optimism in the face of difficulties and your friendliness are among your best assets. Talk it all over with the One Possible She and ask her what she thinks about it.

Key Number 35

WERE you tied to some one's apron-strings too long? Your chief trouble seems to be that you lack self-confidence, for otherwise you are an excellent all-round type. Think over that apron-string matter, however, for it may have rather warped you in several different respects. For one thing, you may still resent the influence that kept you from freely following your own bent when you were younger, and you may have transferred that resentment to other people —whole groups of people. You want to be careful not to hold a subconsciously hostile attitude toward your wife. If you feel irritated when she wants you to polish your shoes, remember that there is nothing at all in that suggestion that ought to make you angry. Your anger is a hang-over from some early resentment.

In more important matters, however, you may give in too easily, but that is because you do not trust your own judgment. Try to be firm where you can dispassionately justify your firmness; and when you yield,

yield without rancor. You should be able to do this, for you have naturally a sunny disposition.

You would probably get along best with a woman who was very much interested in her own affairs, for if she were chiefly interested in yours you would ask her advice one day and resent her interference the next. Get acquainted with many women before you marry. In most respects you should find life easy; your big problem will be your marriage.

Key Number 45

YOU are on rather good terms with life and forgive it the hard blows which it has dealt you. You get more biffs than most men because of your blithe manner of walking straight up to trouble. But you have never learned to cross to the opposite sidewalk when you see temptation coming down the street—even though you know you will wake up with a headache next morning. It doesn't do any good to try to lecture you about doing the things you should not do and leaving undone the things you should do, because you are the only person who can change your personality, and you haven't yet taken the trouble to do so. You answer all criticism with a pleasant smile and agree that the speaker is right.

It is rather a pity that you do not get busy being in reality as efficient as you might be, but so far you have found it too much effort. You have such fine qualities of gaiety, good humor, and light-heartedness. There seems to be no jealousy, envy, rancor, or other mean quality in you. You can get on with almost any man you ever meet. You are not so fortunate with women, but this is because women have a tendency to scold you about your failings. Like most men, you identify your women-folk with your conscience, and both of them speak harsh words to you all too often. So long as you are on bad terms with your conscience—as you are, you know—you will not be comfortable with women. You would better make terms with both of them if you wish to be fully at ease in the world.

Key Number 123

YOU like a thunder-storm, the more thundery the better. You would like to be a part of it; you feel almost as if you were.

It is hard to criticize your type, for your faults are romantic ones, and women love you for them and would not like to see you reform. They like you, too, for your protective ways and the strength which your personality suggests.

You are not a poseur at all, for you are too much interested in what you are doing to think about how you appear to others. You have a strong interest in poetry and art, and it is a sincere one. But you also like practical matters, and business interests you. You would be at your best if you were in some active business that had an artistic or romantic side. In the old days you might have been captain of a whaling ship.

Sensible women like you as much as the flappers do, for you are able to take an interest in them as human beings without always thinking of them as women.

To some extent you consider the world your oyster —and perhaps it is. You are one of the lucky ones in life, deny it though you will.

Key Number 124

FREQUENTLY your wife, or maybe it is your mother or your sweetheart, asks you, "What are you blue about anyway?" You cannot answer her because you do not yourself know. You have most of the things you want or are convinced that you are going to get them in the future, and you take pride and pleasure in your work, your friends, and your possessions. Yet over and over there comes to you the thought that perhaps after all life is hardly worth living.

You have once or twice talked it over with an intimate friend, but he had nothing to offer which you had not already thought of yourself. Probably when you are in such a mood you will get the greatest comfort from the great poets and novelists who have also felt the deep sadness of life and have been able to express it in words instead of in what your friends are accustomed to dub your "grouches."

Fortunately these periods of depression are a minor part of your life. Indeed many of your acquaintances think of you as one of the most genial and light-hearted men they know. You have many

I'VE GOT YOUR NUMBER

friends both among men and among women to whom you are loyal and generous, and you hold your friendships a long time. People in trouble come to you for advice and find you sympathetic. You are an energetic and vigorous worker and do well whether you are working for another person or as your own boss.

Key Number 125

SOME women are always looking for trouble, and you will probably find a wife some day who will not only take the risk of marrying you but will keep right on adoring you in spite of your sins. Let us hope her influence makes you better tempered.

As a matter of fact, if she is the right kind you will have a far happier time than you think you will. Of course people will wonder "how she stands him," and all the girls you did not marry will say how glad of it they are, but after a while the tune will change to "she's done wonders for him" and "he's really not as bad as he used to be" and so on.

One satisfaction you will have in life. People won't overlook you. You are the kind of he-man that attracts men, and whom women, alas, fall madly in love with. You will always be spoiled through life.

Two things, moreover, must be said for you. While you have your ups and downs of temperament, you do not go in for petty criticism; you may swear, but you don't carp. The other thing is that you are no weakling.

A third point for your comfort may be added. You will probably improve as you get older, especially if you see more of women. Seek out the kind that disapproves of you, as well as those romantic young things that are always flocking around you. Get to know strong-minded business women—preferably radicals—who are more interested in themselves than in you. It is not exactly necessary for you to marry that kind; but associate with them, and it will do you a lot of good.

Key Number 134

YOUR friends would be surprised if they knew what goes on in your mind. You live in two worlds, and the second world is marvelous because you made it yourself and in it you are king. Not literally king, because your imagination runs to other lines; perhaps adventurer in far-away lands or beach-comber on a South Sea island or master of industry. You people your second world with your friends, who are many, and wherever you go you carry your Dream Woman with you. No one knows about the Dream Woman, and wild horses could not drag her name out of you. In fact her name changes from time to time, and indeed she is usually a rather vague personality whom you would have a hard time to sketch, but always she is beautiful and kind and ardent and madly in love with you.

Has it ever occurred to you that the reason you do not push ahead faster in your career is because so much of your attention is turned to these beautiful unrealities? They rest you when you are tired; they

cheer you when you are downhearted; but they don't
buy shoes for the baby, and never will. You are ambitious, but you are not going ahead fast enough to
suit you. You will go faster if you can turn your
vivid imagination to actualities. Make your dreams
work for you. Imagination lies back of all achievement. It creates poems, steam-engines, paintings,
weaving-machines, great businesses, new ways of
bookkeeping, time-saving devices, statues, and em-
pires. Are you not somewhat extravagant to use so
much of yours on dreams that can never come true?

Key Number 135

YOU are anxious to be a success and do not hesitate to plunge into a new business, but after you have plunged you begin to question your judgment. Instead of going along on an even keel, you tend to roll somewhat unsteadily. It may be, however, that you will make your big hit some day, when you have given up expecting luck to lift you over the crest of each wave.

Do not hesitate to ask advice from your wife, if you have one. One who does not understand the intimacies of a business can often grasp its needs more readily than an expert who is hampered by his appreciation of minor difficulties.

You are always busy over something and find little time to loaf, but you prefer to do things in your own way. You are more interested in finding a new way to do something than you are in accomplishing a piece of work.

Do not hesitate to face everything squarely, especially the income tax.

Key Number 145

YOU have, or used to have before you were married, the reputation of falling in love with every girl you met and falling out of love with equal facility. Nobody knew about the Fairy Princess whom you have been seeking all your life and have never found. Sometimes you discovered one trait of her in a new acquaintance. This new girl had eyes of the right color, or the right inflection to her voice, or your way of thinking about things. But sooner or later you discovered that she possessed also qualities that no Fairy Princess ever showed. Each time it was a bitter disappointment to you. You never got used to the awakening. You grew cynical and decided that there are no Fairy Princesses among women.

Have you ever stopped to consider that women have the same experience when they look for a Prince Charming among men? We might as well accept the fact that Fairy Princesses and Prince Charmings are never found in the real world. Men and women who would rather be comfortable than broken-hearted make the best of this sad situation and learn to love the boresome, trying, disappointing creatures that human beings really are. If you can join this group of realists, you will find yourself happier in your work and in your human relationships. For you are not always as happy as the people around you believe you to be, since you have a marvelous ability to make others gay when you are most downhearted.

Key Number 234

ONCE they have overcome your slight inertia and persuaded you to go on the picnic, you are the life of the party and the one who makes it a success. You nearly always have a good time, so why do you tend to think at first that you won't go?

Another question: why didn't you make that chicken-coop you planned? Of course it may not have literally been a chicken-coop. Perhaps it was a radio set, but the point is that you wanted to make it and had all the necessary knowledge and then didn't.

The same thing may happen to you in business, so look out for it. You want money, and you ought to seize the opportunity to make it. Otherwise when you see other men moving into big houses and buying big cars you will be dissatisfied.

You are the kind who would use money wisely, for you are generous without being a spendthrift, and you are sensible about your own personal expenditures. You are not particularly interested in "wine, women, and song" as a general principle. (Which

63

does not mean that you don't like women; on the contrary it means that you do—in the most appreciative way.)

You are really rather a dear. The people who brought you up did a good job.

Key Number 235

YOU would be utterly charming and completely satisfactory to yourself as well as others if only you —no, let us leave your only serious defect till the last; so many fine qualities crowd to the front. You always, as the old saying has it, carry a cheerful face. If one were reading your personality in proverbs, one would say you put the right foot out of bed first when you get up. You put that same best foot forward during the day. And, in a final quaint phrase, when you swing your foot, the ball goes. In brief, you are firm on your feet, and marching onward to victory.

You will reach the place you have started for, and you have yourself a pretty clear notion of where that goal is located, although you do not say much about it. You may knock down a few persons who try to stop you, but you are not by nature a cruel person.

But—here is the lack in your character—unless you change your attitude toward women you will not be happy in marriage; no, not though you marry five times. Or seven. You have a profound distrust of women, although they attract you. You can't keep away from them, but you can't get along with them either. Many men are like that. They unconsciously select untrustworthy women and deduce that all are like them, or else they are unconsciously so hostile to women that they stir up hostility in return. You have a good brain, and if you turn intelligence toward this trait, you can correct it. If you do not change your attitude, Heaven help the woman who marries you!

Key Number 245

YOU have so many extraordinarily fine characteristics that you can surely alter the one flaw that is obvious in your personality. Let us talk first about your excellences. You are probably working for some one else. Your answers do not indicate that you have your own business, although this is not quite clear. You have the attributes which qualify a man to climb from one position to another higher and higher until he achieves at last an executive office in which he is responsible to the board of directors alone. You fortunately lack that uneasy quality which makes it necessary for a man to strike out for himself regardless of whether he can succeed or not, because he is unable to coöperate or to accept supervision.

Coöperation is highly developed in you, and you have never hated supervision because you do your work so well. If you are now well along in your career, you will know in your heart that this praise is justified, even though you have not done all that you intended to do. If you are just starting, go on with courage, confident that you will pass many who began the race at the same time with you.

In your business or professional life, you meet chiefly men. This is fortunate, for you have not learned to get along with women satisfactorily. The flaw in your personality is simply a little stupidity in your intelligence. You expect more of women than you do of men, and you are resentful when they fall short of your impossible ideal. If you expect less, you will find that they are not such a bad sort after all.

Key Number 345

YOUR dreams grow as fast as Jack's bean-stalk, forming a strong ladder to which you could mount to reach your goal. Why don't you climb when you are so well fitted to succeed? Instead of getting to the place where you would like to go, you sit at the foot of the bean-stalk which you have planted and dream and wish and lose yourself in fancies.

Perhaps you have never fully realized how much ability you have. You may be the type that takes life easily and needs to be prodded into action. Men like that are apt to marry energetic women who will make them do what they know they ought to do. It is somewhat curious that men who unconsciously choose wives strong in the qualities which they themselves lack are resentful even when they are availing themselves of their wives' strength. They would be much happier if they could admit to themselves that they need and demand the goadings which anger them.

You have the excellent quality of keeping your annoyance to yourself and preserving a cheerful

I'VE GOT YOUR NUMBER

manner when things go against you. You frequently
find it difficult to laugh when your heart is heavy. It
would be a far lighter heart if you could work more
steadily toward your ambitions instead of wishing
they would come true of themselves.

Key Number 1234

ARE you always planning to break away next month? And are you restrained by the feeling that the people who hold you back really know better than you?

If you are still quite young you are probably undecided whether to choose a practical or artistic career, but the artistic will doubtless win, even though you enjoy mechanical things. You will probably develop more between the ages of thirty and forty than between twenty and thirty, the period when most men make their greatest strides.

You have a lovable personality, in spite of being irritable, and a generous spirit toward others. You are extremely sensitive but not touchy. Of course you are always in love.

Your dependence on the people around you comes from your hatred of routine duties. You want others to remind you of them, but you are annoyed when they do.

You might pose a trifle, but fundamentally you are genuine, with real appreciation of subtleties in art, strong ambition, and plenty of character. In literature you like humor, tenderness, and sincerity. You have a most generous admiration for other artists, and a wholesome attitude toward women.

Key Number 1235

WHAT you say goes. What you start you finish. You have little patience with irresolute and lazy persons because you yourself are so self-reliant and energetic. You are the type of man who carries through great enterprises which bring riches to him and more comfort to millions of others. Men of your sort, when they reach the goal toward which they have climbed through long and toilsome years, are often surprised to find how little it means to them after all. The reason for this is that in the stress and strain of the struggle they have not taken time to be considerate and generous toward others. Their minds have been on outwitting their rivals and getting all the work possible out of their employees. Some of them have not even put their attention on making friends of their wives, assuming quite wrongly that once a wife, always a friend.

These are the men who have trouble with their workmen, encounter strikes at crucial points, become involved in lawsuits, and are served with divorce papers. Take thought while there is yet time and cultivate the softer side of your nature. Begin now to greet your acquaintances cordially, to interest yourself sincerely in the lives of your friends, to look upon women as friendly creatures, to speak words of admiration instead of criticism, and to give generous praise where it is due. Do not forget that recreation in its place is as important as industry and ambition.

Key Number 1245

WHAT a lot of energy you waste! Some of it goes into disliking people; some of it goes into planning schemes that you have not the slightest intention of carrying out; and some of it goes into carrying out impulses that are futile. You really do not care about the things you do or do the things you care about.

And yet, in spite of all this, you have great strength of character. You are hard to influence—for good or evil. Stubborn? If you ever had an argument with a mule, you'd win.

So just face yourself and admit that something ought to be done about it. Admit that that girl who recently told you a few plain truths about yourself was right! You have so much strength that you can afford to be gentle. To yield now and then would not make you weaker in the eyes of the world, but stronger, more lovable.

Of course you might feel that your impregnable citadel had been taken if you ever let any one gain your confidence, but provided it were the right person you would be happier afterward. For you want to be liked—more than you will admit to yourself. But let your friendships have something more than an emotional basis; for that way, for you, lies disillusionment.

Key Number 1345

THE people who call you vacillating and fickle do not know what they are talking about. You only seem so to those who do not understand you. You might as well accept the fact that the majority never will realize the sort of a person you are, for you have an unusual combination of qualities. Perhaps one woman loves you enough to bear with your many trying traits for the sake of something fine which she vaguely feels is there; maybe that woman is waiting for you somewhere in the future. But you have a most unfortunate tendency to show the worst side of your personality at times when it does you the most harm. This is a part of a contrariness of your nature, and it makes it very hard for any woman to bear with you. You blame the unfortunate outcome on the woman, and sometimes it may be her fault; but usually it is because you draw too heavily on the patience, affection, and comprehension of any one with whom you are closely associated.

All this hurts you deeply, and you sometimes resolve to go away and live utterly alone, where you will not be so constantly disappointed in people. Is one of your favorite day-dreams of a desert island with all the comforts of home but no relatives?

You know your own faults better than any one else, although you have not realized how unhappy they have made you. Choose the opposite of the trait that makes you the most trouble and develop this new characteristic. If you like the result, try the same recipe on other phases of your personality.

CHARACTER STUDIES FOR MEN

Key Number 2345

YOURS is a rather curious character combining some almost contradictory traits. You have the business man's temperament and the poet's heart, for one thing. Part of the time you seem like a typical hustler who will make the Rotary Club early; then you suddenly begin to wonder if you would not rather give it all up and go off to the South Seas, or some equally distant spot. You know few women really well; perhaps none at all. You have any number of acquaintances but tend to keep on the surface with them, and it hardly occurs to you that women have their problems just as you have. It is just possible that you have two conceptions of women: the imaginary woman, to whom you could open your heart; and the real woman, to whom you have given very little attention. You think you understand her of course, but that is only because you assume that there is nothing intricate about her.

With men you are more communicative and very popular, especially in your buoyant moods. You are

79

apt to overwork, though, and when you are tired you get discouraged.

Beware the influence of moonlight! Let both your selves sit in conference before undertaking anything important. In other words, be sure that what you do appeals as reasonable to the practical side of you, and also let it satisfy that part of you that wants more out of life than worldly success.

Key Number 12345

YOU have the qualities that make for spectacular success, but you are not happy. Probably your dejection does not show, for you are not the kind to wail your sorrows to the crowd. You share your gaiety and keep your depression to yourself.

You are likely to be one of the most important men of your community by the time you are forty, for you can see what should be done, make plans for accomplishing it, and direct other men. You are better as a promoter than as a day-by-day executive. You are always thinking up new plans, and sometimes you want to upset affairs that are going very well in order to experiment with making them go better. You get sat on by your superiors when you make such suggestions. You lose heart then and swear to yourself that you never again will attempt to beat sense into their brains, and you fall into a black mood and hate the world.

You are drawn to women, but because you distrust them you are always at odds with them, and that adds to your unhappiness. If you could only accept bosses and women as a part of the scheme of life, and adjust yourself to their deficiencies, since you cannot change them, you would save yourself many a heartache. Some of the schemes which you have put through with enormous effort would have gone easily if you had studied more carefully the personalities with which you had to deal.

QUESTIONS FOR WOMEN

For directions see page 1

GROUP 1

A—Would you like to go up in an airplane?

B—If you heard a noise at night would you get up to investigate it?

C—Are you among "the first by whom the new is tried"?

D—Would you paint your house bright blue if you felt like it?

E—Would you interfere with a woman who was slapping her baby on the street?

GROUP 2

A—Do you get hysterical?

B—Would you walk five blocks to see a parade?

C—Do you cry at the theater?

D—Do many people "get on your nerves"?

E—Do you have strong likes and dislikes?

GROUP 3

A—Do you avoid asking advice if possible?

B—Do you object to giving in for the sake of peace?

C—Are your mistakes your own fault?

D—Do you read what you like rather than what you are told you should?

E—Does achievement gratify you more than admiration?

GROUP 4

A—Do you prefer to make a decision rather than "wait to see what breaks"?

B—Are you as successful as your friends?

C—Do you trust your own judgment?

D—Can you forget your social "breaks"?

E—Do you answer these questions easily rather than tend to quibble?

GROUP 5

A—If a woman you dislike is wearing a becoming hat, are you willing to tell her so?

B—Do you like three of the last five people you talked with? (Present company excepted.)

C—Do you like most of your friends' friends?

D—Do you think the world is growing better?

E—Do you tell white lies to make people happy?

KEY NUMBERS FOR WOMEN

0	see page	97	123	" "	129
1	" "	99	124	" "	131
2	" "	101	125	" "	133
3	" "	103	134	" "	135
4	" "	105	135	" "	137
5	" "	107	145	" "	139
12	" "	109	234	" "	141
13	" "	111	235	" "	143
14	" "	113	245	" "	145
15	" "	115	345	" "	147
23	" "	117	1234	" "	149
24	" "	119	1235	" "	151
25	" "	121	1245	" "	153
34	" "	123	1345	" "	155
35	" "	125	2345	" "	157
45	" "	127	12345	" "	159

CHARACTER STUDIES FOR WOMEN

Key Number 0

THERE is no blinking the fact that you are an old-fashioned clinging vine, and it is very lucky for you that a large proportion of men still prefer that sort. If you have married a man who wants a sturdy oak of a wife, you are out of luck, my dear; and the best you can do is to endure the situation in the quiet, placid manner which is your greatest charm.

If you are not yet married, look for a man who will be a kind protector and a good provider. If you do not marry, get yourself into a steady job where faithfulness and industry count for more than aggressiveness, for there is not in you one half-ounce of that disquieting quality called ambition.

Now, here is a gentle warning. A woman who relies on others as much as you do must find a way of repaying the debt she owes. No, keeping the house and spanking the children is not enough. She must pay in gratitude and love. She must learn to say aloud all the kind thoughts that come into her mind while she keeps critical remarks from coming out. A clinging vine may be poison ivy, or it may be honeysuckle, yielding up fragrance to the whole garden.

97

Key Number 1

YOU are most fortunate in your philosophical temperament and your calmness in what would be to others an occasion for hysteria. High-strung men are particularly attracted to you on this account. But it is possible that you are too limited in your friendships. If you were less sensitive to people's bad qualities you could more enjoy their excellences.

Your greatest handicap is lack of belief in yourself. You overestimate the ability of others, thus underestimating yourself. Those on whom you can lean may have less actual stability than you have. Try standing on your own feet. Get an impersonal view of your characteristics and let the admirable ones be an incentive to improving the poorer ones. Your finest quality is your courage. This is the engine that will pull you over sandy roads of monotony, through swamps of despair, up hills of difficulty, until you finally reach a height from which you behold a glorious future.

Key Number 2

YOU are something of a dreamer, seeing yourself in the glamorous atmosphere of fame or luxury, the center of all eyes, the adored one of a countless throng of admirers. Next time you find yourself slipping into that dream, why not ask yourself how you are going to bring it about? Are you planning to marry the Prince of Wales? That would certainly give you the prominence you would like to enjoy, but as a practical solution of your problems it has its limitations. Suppose you try something easier; not marriage necessarily, for perhaps you would be just as happy unmarried, but something that would bring beauty into your life. For you are a beauty lover.

As a matter of fact, in spite of your dreams you are not really ambitious; you would like to be famous, or else a woman of wealth, living in luxury in vast palatial rooms, but not if it involves doing something about it. Perhaps, after all, you enjoy your dreams as much as you would their fulfilment. The ambitious ones seldom have dreams that they cannot conceivably realize; the dreamers seldom confine themselves to dreams that they can make come true. Only a woman who is very charming is likely to develop a personality of the kind you seem to have.

Key Number 3

A FAVORITE grievance that we hear expressed every time a new invention comes into the home is: "I was born fifty years too soon." But you were born fifty years too late! Can you not see yourself as a pioneer woman going stanchly on to face the things you fear? Perhaps it is this grim realization that life must be grappled with, hardship endured, and fears overcome that makes you a little out of sympathy with the flippancies and frivolities of the present generation. Dancing girls seem to you like butterflies on the edge of a volcano; to you gilded youth in motor-cars seems to be steering headlong for a precipice.

Have you sometimes wished that you were a man, with the thought that then your gift for organization would be given free play? If this is the case, you are using your sex as an excuse for failure. As a matter of fact you have fewer handicaps to overcome on the road to success than most of us, for you get your way rather easily. You do not have to go into hysterics over it either; in fact hysterics are not in your line, and you have no interest in staging a scene in which you would play the chief rôle.

It is probable, in fact, that you have already achieved a good deal. You have learned to stand on your own feet and to be independent; in short, you have learned to grow up when you would have preferred to remain a protected child. The rôle of the pioneer woman suits you chiefly because you would like to have been the protected wife of the pioneer man. You would have admired his courage, resourcefulness, strength, and manliness; and you would have liked to direct him, just as you would like to drive an engine. You would rather spur others on to courageous deeds than do them yourself. But remember that if you want your husband to be a pioneer man it is a rather selfish desire on your part. It might be very much better for you if he were quite the opposite. But not for him!

Key Number 4

YOU begin every piece of work superbly. The master mind and the craftsman's hand are both yours. Your comrades admire you frantically—for a little while. You slump in the very middle of your achievement because you are bored and something new attracts your attention. Again your start is magnificent; again you don't hold out. The plodding tortoise seldom finds you at the goal you could so easily have reached. You do not realize that it is this characteristic which has caused you so much trouble. You blame other people for your failures. You have all the qualities that make for success except staying-power.

When your type goes in for marriage, the number of husbands is greater than the number of golden weddings.

The lack of completion in any phase of your life is what makes you so restless. Sometimes a woman like you is eaten up by jealousy of much inferior women who have got ahead by sticking to one line. Only by turning your energy toward one aim and holding to that will you find your rightful satisfaction in life.

Key Number 5

A GREAT many people expect special concessions from the world because they suffer from shyness, sensitiveness, and a retiring disposition. They want to be taken care of like children after they have grown up. They do not trust their own judgment.

The whole success or failure of your future life depends on your getting rid of the feeling that you are not as good as your neighbor. Because you are exceptionally just by nature, you have leaned over backward in giving others their due. Your own sincerity has made you blind to the fact that the showiness of many people who impress you as successful is a large bluff. You should learn to ignore everything about yourself that is unfavorable and concentrate on your good qualities, which far outnumber your weaknesses. Think of all the kindly things you have done during the past year. Think of the faithful way in which you have kept all your promises, whether other people were doing their share or not.

Think of your good points continually so that you

completely forget the diffidence that is holding you back. (The fact that you frequently tell yourself that you are superior to your neighbors in certain respects —perhaps mentally or socially—is only another manifestation of your sense of inferiority. Do not dwell so much on your superiority, but forget your inferiority.) Incidentally, your appearance is probably far more attractive than you think it is.

Decide what you wish to do, make practical plans for doing it, and then take the first steps regardless of whether you expect to succeed or not. Walk straight up to the job even if it is failure that awaits you. If you always have to carry doubt and worry on your back, you will find the burden a severe handicap, and it will not excuse you from bearing your part in the world's work.

Key Number 12

ALTHOUGH you at first appear easy to get along with, you do not care for the average person. You prefer a few close friends to many acquaintances. This of course has its advantages, but are you not making the mistake of sheltering yourself from the world too much? Do not your prejudices keep you from seeing that every one has something to give you and something to receive from you, in spite of a few unlovely traits that force themselves on your attention? You would be less lonely if you tempered your critical judgments with compassion.

Strangely enough one of your best qualities is usually considered a failing—your unstable and excitable temperament. While as a rule emotionalism is no virtue, yet this trait shows that you are alive and alert. Temper your high spirit with kindliness, and you will find that instead of making lines in your face, it will come out as vivacity instead of irritation. Seek out all humanizing influences—dogs or cats, if you like them, flowers, the theater, music, or out-of-door life. By all means buy a new frock if you feel like it. Try to make yourself happy, not spasmodically happy, but daily and hourly more serene. If you will face the facts—as you probably will, for you are almost a Spartan in courage—you will probably admit that it is only when you are happy yourself that you really want to see others happy.

Key Number 13

WOMEN like you are sometimes more unhappy because of their good qualities than on account of their faults, for your excellences are those which society admires in a man and resents in a woman. You are like Napoleon leading his troops into battle, like a great doctor fighting a pestilence, but you are a complete failure as a flapper or a member of a church sewing-circle. Two courses lie open to you: either accept your destiny of being different from the popular model of woman, or make peace with the world by developing conscientiously the feminine side of your nature—courtesy, interest in others, kindness, and like qualities that belong both to a gentlewoman and to a perfect gentle knight.

The latter course—that of being as much like women as you conveniently can—has the advantage because every one hates to be obviously different. The resentment which comes between you and other individuals is anger at their attitude toward your outspoken aggressiveness. If you can cultivate the so-called womanly traits, women and more especially men will cease to fear you and will admire your forthrightness.

Key Number 14

YOU are willing to bear your share of the burdens of life; and you do not ask in return, as so many do, for a blare of trumpets to precede you. Your fortitude helps you to carry on when you would much rather rest. But while you do not want to lead, neither do you especially like to see others lead. You are not the first to applaud the general as he rides by in glory; indeed you are rather grudging when it comes to giving others their due. It would not hurt you to praise people a little more. You will find that it makes you feel more warmly toward them and it makes them feel more warmly toward you.

You desire independence, but you do not fight for it. You trust your own judgment but do not follow it. You have the courage of your convictions but are too indifferent to do anything about it.

Men do not mean as much to you as they do to the average woman; yet in spite of your cold-heartedness you are rather attractive to men, especially in business relations. They know that they can depend upon you.

I'VE GOT YOUR NUMBER

You would do well to make more friends and really try to keep them. You are in danger of becoming too introspective and too indifferent to other people. Remember, those who are popular have to work for their popularity, not once, but every day of their lives.

Key Number 15

CAN you make a decision? Or do you allow others to decide for you? It looks as if that were your weakest point—a tendency to lean on others' judgment, a willingness to let others guide your life. A girl of this type is in danger of remaining under her parents' control too long, allowing them to choose her husband for her or even to discourage a perfectly good suitor because they want to keep her at home.

A woman with your traits makes the best possible sort of a wife for a strong-willed, adventurous, affectionate man. You would follow your husband without hesitation to icebergs or deserts or jungles and count the comforts of civilization well lost if only you could be with him.

You do not make much show of your affections, deep as they are. You are perhaps a little too placid, although that quality is a restful one on which highstrung natures enjoy leaning. You are a tigress protecting her cubs when your loved ones are menaced, and since your love is broad and generous there are many who call you blessed.

Key Number 23

WHAT are you afraid of anyway? Mice and men and thunder-storms, or poverty and sickness and unknown misfortunes? Snap your finger at the first group and be philosophical about the others, for worry summons troubles about you as a dinner-bell calls summer boarders to a meal. I will say this for you: you tackle life vigorously, but Old Man Worry sits on your shoulders and chuckles because he makes the struggle so hard for you. The problems of work and love and bringing up children and getting comfortable shoes that aren't too ugly are difficult enough without having half one's energy diverted into chronic anxiety.

Do you know that sometimes a woman is able to make a dark emotion over into a feeling as glorious as the sun at midday? There was once a woman who only partly liked her husband. The part she did not like grew bigger and bigger, and the part she did like became a dwarf. Something had to be done, and this is what she did. She made out a list of her husband's good qualities and of every advantage she gained by being married to him. She read that list over and over as if it were the prayer-book every time she felt hateful toward him. By the time the paper wore out something very curious had happened: she had fallen in love with her husband! She discovered that the man with whom she had been living for fifteen years was an entirely different person from what she had supposed, and that she adored him.

Key Number 24

ONCE in a while you feel that you ought to make a speech. Perhaps you have a chance to make it to the public; if so, you are fortunate, and so is your family. Of course you are frightened to death at making speeches, but you do it because you feel that you can make a speech as well as anybody; and so why shouldn't you? You feel that you are right in what you have to say, and so why shouldn't people listen to you?

They should, but before you make your speeches (whether formal or informal) be sure to marshal all your facts. Find out beforehand just what the other person's point of view is, so that when he presents it you will have your answer ready. Put yourself in his place, and see all the reason that you can in his arguments, so that your answer will convince rather than annoy him.

You are usually ready to take up arms for your friends, which is an endearing quality, but be sure that partizanship does not overbalance your judgment. If you could spread your feeling thin so that it would cover more people and be less intense, it might be better for you.

Your energy and quick championship of the oppressed make you a person who will be appreciated in an hour of need. By the way, you may be glad to hear that you are the type of woman who gets an unusually nice husband.

Key Number 25

DID you ever know a woman who was so fond of her children that she could not let them have a good time? That may be your danger. And then, when they break away, as they must, how lost you will feel! Please try not to hold so tightly to your loved ones, because you do it not only to save them from danger, but also to save yourself from feeling lost. Remember it is only children who get panicky when they find themselves alone. You should train yourself to look your fears in the eye, and they will slink away.

The root of your trouble is that you do not appreciate yourself. You would rather be guided than lead. And yet you have such splendid qualities, such unselfish impulses and ready sympathy, and such unexpected energy in helping those who are in trouble. It gives you great satisfaction, does it not, to feel that some life has been made happier through your efforts? Probably, for one thing, you are something of a match-maker, and like nothing better than to watch your deep-laid schemes blossom.

I'VE GOT YOUR NUMBER

Your chief charm is a childlike trusting spirit which makes people want to protect you. And you dress to suit the part. You have an April temperament, balmy one minute and stormy the next. If you will learn by experience that most of your fears are unfounded, and face the world a little more courageously, you will find that it is more satisfactory to live your own life than to be an accessory—however valuable—of some other life. Good luck to you!

Key Number 34

WHERE other people are afraid, you go ahead confidently, although you get panicky over simple matters not worth noticing. You really cannot be classified either as a brave woman or as a coward, because you jump from one side to the other so fast. If you could only mix the two traits you would be just right.

Your poise and your way of going ahead in the direction you choose are fine; but are you not a little inclined to elbow others out of the way? It may be true that they are blocking progress, but be a little more patient with them, for they can't help being blockheads.

You are a curious mixture of traits all jumbled up together. Some of your finest characteristics have been pushed into the background by your passion for getting ahead—shall one say for having your own way? Bring forward your generosity, comprehension of others, altruism, and high ideals, and be the woman that only you can be.

Key Number 35

NOBODY guesses how hard it sometimes is for you to keep on "doing the next thing." Often it seems to you as if life rose up against you like a tidal wave. You shut your eyes and hold your breath, and after eons of smothering desolation you find yourself on the crest, not broken but triumphant. Were you a hysterical woman you would long ago have gone under.

It is strange that you have never learned the lesson of self-confidence from your many victories. Count up your successes and forget your failures. You present a valiant front, and no one sees that you are really trembling. The tragedy is that there is no need for your uneasiness. You will always surmount the wave.

Love of your family and of your wide circle of friends is the motive that inspires most of your actions. You express this devotion more in deeds than in words, and this has given you something of a reputation for being cold. If you can bring yourself to be more demonstrative, people will immediately begin to be drawn to you and sing loudly praises of the real You.

Key Number 45

MOST people like you, although you are not fault-less! You lack the inspiring rushes of enthusiasm that would carry you over difficulties, but on the other hand you never throw fits when you are displeased. Indeed you are not easily annoyed; you take life calmly on the whole. One hopes you are married, for you are the type who loves her children but does not let them put anything over on her. You have enough timidity to give a husband the sense of protecting you, but you will never be a burden.

You are efficient and adaptable, not self-willed; ready to let others make the decisions, and able to adjust yourself to their wishes. You know your good qualities, and this gives you confidence. If you work for a living you will probably reach a moderately high position, for you are not afraid to tackle new tasks; but not the highest, for you lack aggressiveness. The other workers in the office will like you and have a tendency to let you help them too much. Be on your guard against allowing yourself to be drawn into other people's affairs. If you made your decisions more firmly and showed more energy in bringing the good things of life your way, you would be very nearly an ideal woman.

Key Number 123

Do you eat the candied cherry on the top of the cake first or save it till the last? At the end of this discourse you will find a plump red cherry, but first comes a fault that you should correct. You have not allowed your sympathies and your affections to flow in a broad deep stream toward the people who make up your neighborhood, your city, your nation, your world. You have vigorous emotions. You could be a great lover. Instead it sometimes seems as if you were in training to be a great hater! Your lack of outgoing love may be due to a feeling that you have not a fair share of comfort, good times, talents, social position, and happiness. You may be bitter toward those who have more.

You possess two fine traits that should bring you satisfaction: you are strong and courageous. That is the cherry I promised you—two cherries—strength and courage. A woman who has those characteristics is able to cope with any situation. She can make herself all over. You can, if you choose, become the finest of human beings—a woman whose love goes round the world and reaches to the stars above.

Key Number 124

You are not one to yearn for things that you can buy around the corner. If you want anything, you usually go and get it—at least you *decide* to go and get it. Your weakness is not indecision, but the lack of initiative to carry out your decisions.

Do you tend to look down on the mass of humanity? Do you wish the world were made up of "fewer and better people"? Have you ever so far fallen from grace as to think of a crowd of people as "cattle"? If you have, it is clear that the thing which keeps you from realizing the best that is in you is indifference. You have not sufficiently used your imagination on other people, each one of whom can be a sympathetic character if you can look at him from the proper angle.

You have splendid qualities otherwise: readiness to face an issue, plenty of warmth (but focused on a few persons) and—oh, rare virtue!—the ability to look at others through level eyes that are not lifted in admiration. If you fall into the opposite fault of looking down on those whom you consider beneath you, it is a fault easier to overcome.

Key Number 125

HAVE you ever wondered why it is that you do things for others which you would never think of doing for yourself? You would beg, borrow, almost steal for a loved one, while you can hardly bring yourself to accept the necessities of life from another's hand.

The reason is simple. You have not a very high opinion of yourself, in spite of all the pleasant words people say of you, and you have a guilty feeling that you haven't any right to the good things of life. So you enjoy them through getting them for your friends and family or any one who needs help. You are applying a cure to an emotional sickness from which you suffer—the sickness of self-depreciation, of lack of confidence, poise, and self-reliance. You gain a justifiable pride and sense of power in "helping lame dogs over the stile." Keep doing this, but to your philanthropy add a little attention to yourself. If you are married, get your husband to unite with you in budgeting the income, so that a definite amount will be spent on your clothes. If you are a wage-earner, set yourself to win a higher salary or a better position. If you are unmarried, see how many men you can make propose to you in the next year, but don't marry more than one of them.

Key Number 134

NOW you are about to be told, straight off the bat, what you have to guard against. Don't be annoyed, please. If you are not very careful indeed, you are going to steam-roller your friends, family, and the other committee members.

You do things so easily and efficiently that people instinctively turn to you for advice and help. In your eagerness to aid, you are likely to try to make them do what is good for them instead of encouraging them to do what they want to do.

If you were a man you would be a master of industry or a political boss, and everything would be all right. But you are a woman, and it will avail you little to make your home as lovely as a bower of roses, as neat as a pin, and as regular as clockwork, if you boss your family. For people will be hostile, and that cuts you. And, oh, be very, very careful about your husband who is or is to be! He may resent your positive character even while he admires it. Look for his strong points, and let him lead half the time. You may have then the most wonderful form of love—the love of married comrades.

Key Number 135

YOU are one of those who desire to protect humanity, but whose sphere of influence is limited by your own inability to express the loving-kindness that is one of your fundamental traits. Wise, strong, and generous, you lack only the initiative and self-confidence to undertake the things you plan.

Do not let the pleasure of looking down on yourself impair the dignity of your soul; do not refuse to admit your own intrinsic merits. For you are the kind whose influence is needed. Though you may seem to others a trifle cold and forbidding, you have a compassionate heart and a stanch spirit. Free from emotionalism, you can look fairly at any question that does not involve an estimate of your own personality. Your good-will and kindliness will carry you farther than the spasmodic warmth that you probably admire so much in others.

You are inclined to be shy, but you have the courage of your convictions when your sense of justice is outraged, and you can come to the front with the best of them.

I'VE GOT YOUR NUMBER

Some people believe in the theory that each person is at his or her best at a certain age and in one or another of the human relationships. If this is true, you would probably be at your best between the ages of thirty and forty. Your best qualities are the kind that would be most apparent in middle life, and your most successful rôle will be that of mother. This is indeed a rare trait.

Key Number 145

A PICTURE of you might be called "Lady with a Clear Conscience." It would show you with a gentle mouth somewhat contradicted by resolute eyes. It would show you with a calm brow and a feminine chin. It would show you as the kind of woman who is called "easy-going," except when a moral issue is involved. Then, roused from your natural calm, you take matters into your own hand and call up the S.P.C.A. or do whatever else is necessary.

You would be at your best as a married woman, but you are not necessarily the kind that marries early. Your traits do not appeal so much to young men as to older ones. Children like you, and you would make an excellent teacher. If you have any children you will find them easy to manage if they are like you rather than like their father, for the kind of man you pick out will have a will of his own. It is just as well that you have plenty of self-control.

You are not afraid to carry out your own ideas be-

139

cause you are sure that they are right, but you would prefer to have some one else do the actual work. When people are in trouble, however, you are among the first to offer consolation and practical suggestions. You doubtless had a pleasant home during your childhood and were proud of your parents. You admire your husband too, if you have one; indeed your domestic relations have always been harmonious. Perhaps this is because your character shows the somewhat rare combination of self-confidence, a generous spirit, and a disposition to see the other person's point of view.

Key Number 234

Dɪᴅ it ever occur to you that as a free and independent adult you can do pretty much as you like? Instead of fighting others, why do you not go ahead and do what you want to do? As a matter of fact there are two reasons why you don't: first, because the plans you want to carry out are plans for other people as well as for yourself, and they have their own ideas about what is best for them; and, second, because you are afraid to follow your own advice. You feel sure that your ideas are good, yet you can be dissuaded from carrying them out, and then, when it is proved that you were right after all, you want to blame those who held you back.

You have a vivid personality and make yourself felt. You are dominant and self-confident; both are excellent qualities if accompanied by good judgment and a friendly feeling toward others. If you are a little inclined to look at yourself as the center of the universe, it is only because you are very much interested in yourself, and that is commendable. But try once in a while to think of other persons as the heroes and heroines of their own stories, and it may help you to gain a more tender human spirit.

Even though you have abundant energy, you waste too much of it in fighting individuals both in your home and out of it. Windmills may look like enemies, but they are really quite harmless.

Key Number 235

YOU sound as if you were a trifle timid, though I cannot see why a woman of your personality should ever doubt herself. Of course you make mistakes, but most mistakes are not really very serious, and a large number of them can be corrected. Why do you distrust your ability to deal with life?

People are fond of you. Confess they are, although they may sometimes tell you that your heart runs away with your head, and that you are looking for trouble, and they may give you sage advice that worries you because you have no intention of following it.

Finest of all your traits is the way your interest goes out to others, so that what happens to them is almost as if it happened to you. The pleasures that come to you you cannot enjoy unless you share them.

On second thoughts, I believe that even that fine characteristic is not so admirable as the way you go ahead along what you think is the right course in spite of doubts and worries. I take back what I said about your timidity, for you advance when you are afraid, and that is the greatest courage of all.

Key Number 245

You have been exceptionally fortunate in your early training. Traits that might have handicapped you are for the most part buried, and you face the world with assurance.

Very affectionate, friendly toward the neighbors, and demonstrative toward those at home, you are the kind of woman who is usually considered an "ideal wife" because of the warm atmosphere which you create and the efficiency of your management.

Your greatest weakness is a certain timidity, physical rather than mental, due perhaps to a too comfortable environment and sheltered life. This does not, however, indicate in your case any tendency to retire to the background. Perhaps you have yourself noticed the contradictory characteristics that make you sometimes lead and at other times run away from situations that call for courageous handling.

Key Number 345

HOW nice you are to your friends! You love to invite them to tea and plan little surprises for them, and you are very likely to remember their birthdays. Usually you appear as the perfect hostess, calmly at ease, but you yourself know that your smile sometimes conceals a heartache. It is not so much things that have happened that disturb you, as the things that you fear may happen. You are always anxious about the health and safety of those who are dearest to you.

Your affections are strongly centered perhaps on one person, and you are willing to sacrifice others for the sake of the loved one.

You have aptitude for business but probably prefer a sheltered life. Your moral standards are high, and you are not afraid to stand up for what you believe is right. But are you not something of a pussycat when it comes to staying home by the fire? But, then, there is no reason to go out into the wind and rain unless you have an adventurous spirit—or an unhappy home. And yours is likely to be happy, for people like you who want to make other people happy are very likely to succeed.

Key Number 1234

NOTHING will surprise you more than to hear of your worst fault, for very likely you have always thought of the opposite trait as your greatest virtue. In spite of the fact that you are of a warm emotional temperament, in spite of the wideness of your circle of friends, you cannot be put down as "one who loves his fellow-men." In flashes you think of the man in the street as your friend, but for the most part he means less to you than a tree. You are, however, exceptionally fond of trees. Very likely there is something about trees among the poems you have written.

It is hard to give sufficient praise to your fine qualities, the decisiveness of character that will bring you success, your fearless attitude toward the world, and your appreciation of the worth-while things of life. You are generous, too, and like to do the treating. But your generosity is rather impulsive. You help the weak because they are weak, not because you love them. You do not yourself worry, nor understand people who do.

I'VE GOT YOUR NUMBER

If you are married, or thinking of getting married, remember that your husband is a personality as well as a husband. For except for that rather alarming, and rather fascinating, savage streak and tendency to know everything, you are a really fine woman. You do not realize yourself how near you come to being ideal.

Key Number 1235

POOR thing! You think you have to "grin and bear it." Not that you are afraid to cut the ties that bind you, but you are too tender-hearted to risk hurting people's feelings. Also you want to be loved, and you think that the way to be loved is to be docile. Yours is a peculiarly strong and fine character, with all the qualities to make a happy successful woman, except that you feel obliged to accept what life gives you. You are too polite to Life. (Were you, perhaps, brought up with an undue emphasis on politeness?)

As you grow older, things are sure to improve for you, for as your character strengthens you will begin to see that there is no reason why you should endure hardship. If you have the strength for endurance, you have the strength for action, and in few cases is endurance necessary. Remember it is not courage you lack so much as self-confidence.

Your home life is very happy or very unhappy or both alternately; for your affections are strong, and yet you want to be free—a difficult combination.

I'VE GOT YOUR NUMBER

Your business life, if you have one, ought to be more serene and very successful. You have the qualities that make women succeed in business, which, by the way, are feminine qualities. You are not envious, and your outlook is wholesome. You think rightly, or pleasantly, on most subjects. You are cheerful, popular, and optimistic, especially on the surface. You do not waste much time thinking about your enemies.

You are extremely popular with men, and also with women. And that means a great deal. For when both men and women agree on a person there is little chance for argument.

Key Number 1245

YOU have many warm friends and a few warm enemies, for yours is a type that people respond to strongly either one way or the other. At least you never need be afraid of being disregarded!

You have the courage of your convictions, and the only danger is that your convictions may not be sound. Perhaps you should ask advice more, even though you hate to do it. If you were not such a distinctly feminine type (with such a feminine method of getting your own way), you might be called dominating; as it is, people are usually indulgent toward you where they would be resentful toward other women who went ahead as you do. But they know that you have a warm heart, and they admire your courage.

Your danger, of course, is that some day you will upset the apple-cart by a sudden burst of temper. The thing you should guard against is nervousness, and the way to control that is to rest. You probably say that you cannot rest, but any one can say that. If

I'VE GOT YOUR NUMBER

you overwork, you have to rest in the end, somewhere or somehow, for you can't tax nature beyond her strength. Isn't it better to plan wisely when and where you will rest, instead of letting circumstances decide it for you?

Key Number 1345

NOTHING gets on your nerves. You can work under handicaps that would make the average woman rise in wrath and leave the house. If your gifts are mental, you are the type that might be very successful on a college faculty, where your ability and calm temperament would make you a real force. If, on the other hand, it is chiefly in your home that you shine, you are even more fortunate, for once your interest is centered on your home you can make it a home to be proud of. But do not try to be both a business woman and a home-maker. If you have a career before you, give some one else the housework to do— or it won't get done.

Perhaps your finest trait is loyalty. Your natural desire is to like people and to keep on liking them as long as you possibly can. You are distinctly disappointed when they fall short of what you thought they were.

If it were not for your loving heart there might be the danger that you would dominate your husband, but your common sense and natural generosity have doubtless steered you away from this danger. There are few people who can equal you in the traits that make up a fine, firm, and courageous character softened by the magic of kindliness.

Key Number 2345

PEOPLE go to you for sympathy, for yours is not only whole-souled but made practical by your faculty for discriminating criticism and sound advice. If you are still in your early twenties or younger you are probably popular with the boys, for you are not an unreasonable creature who has to be kept in a good temper. Although you have a chin of your own, you are willing to allow other people to have chins too; in fact in an emergency you are only too glad to have some one around who can help you through.

You like a good time so much that in order to get it you can overcome some of the little-girl fears that you have not quite outgrown. Try to do that, for timidity is one of your very few weaknesses.

Domesticity appeals to you, but so does a career. The only thing that would worry you in undertaking a new venture would be the thought that some power which you could not control might upset your plans. You do not distrust your own judgment or your own ability, but you are nervous about possible accidents.

I'VE GOT YOUR NUMBER

Be careful not to marry some one who wants to rediscover the North Pole. You never could settle down to your own work if your husband were far away.

Key Number 12345

ONE question you should ask yourself: have you emotional balance, or does your heart guide your life without enough help from your brain? Your answers do not indicate whether or not you have the common sense which holds good qualities from overdoing. For you have heaps and piles and mountains of desirable traits. Beneath a completely feminine appearance you hide manly strength and determination. Your husband was (or will be) surprised the first time he ran (or runs) against your insistence that he should (or shall) do what he knew he ought to do and did not like to. Nothing but your great love and slightly tardy tact will save the situation.

You must always be on your guard against domineering over the weaker personalities that flock to you like homeless dogs. It will be a temptation to hold on to your children after they have grown up. Learn to express your generous love through letting people make their own mistakes, and do not come into the matter till they appeal to you to have their hurts kissed away with understanding and admiration.

159 (21)

I've Got Your Number!
Second Series

QUESTIONS FOR MEN

(Answer the questions yourself; do not let others answer for you.)

GROUP 1

A—Do you accept yourself as you are, without trying to improve your character?

B—Is it all right for a boy to lie to get his dog out of trouble?

C—Have you a good swearing vocabulary?

D—Does the Boy Scout slogan "Do a good deed every day" grate on you?

E—Is it all right for a man to kiss a married woman in private if he can get away with it?

GROUP 2

A—Can you refuse a second helping which you do not want if your hostess presses it upon you?

B—Would you rather go by a much longer route than turn back when you have made a mistake in the road?

C—Would you hold out against the other eleven men on the jury?

D—Does criticism of your plans often give you an impetus to go ahead?

E—Do you keep your resolutions?

GROUP 3

A—Does it amuse you to see a man miss his train?

B—Would you ever try to make a woman jealous if you were sure of her affection?

C—Is it good policy to keep business away from a competitor even if you cannot fill the order yourself?

D—Would the average boy drown a puppy for a dollar?

E—A group of people of all ages were dancing the Paul Jones at a club. When the change of partners came a man realized that the only girl left without a partner was an unattractive one whom he disliked. He could fade away before she saw him. Was he justified in doing this?

GROUP 4

A—Do you hope our present form of government will continue indefinitely?

B—Would you rather deal with an old established firm than with an energetic new one, if no other considerations were involved?

C—Would you hate to see colored evening clothes for men introduced, if no expense were involved?

D—Do you dislike the fashion of girls wearing shorts?

E—Do you like to keep up old traditions, even if they are somewhat inconvenient?

GROUP 5

A—Are you bored by the love-scenes in the movies?

B—Can you say that you have never bullied a woman?

C—Do you prefer a march to sentimental music?

D—Can you say that women are never jealous of one another because of you?

E—Do you receive more compliments on your personality and character than on your looks?

15

KEY NUMBERS FOR MEN

Key Number 0

YOU are a man of moods. Sometimes you eat raw meat and drink blood. Other days your spirit slinks in dark corners. But you never do anything mean. You cannot harden your heart to a woman or close your ears to adventure's call. The sirens and the Loreleis will get you if you don't watch out, and how you will repent when the fun is all over! For your conscience is a tardy alarm-clock that wakes you after the train is gone, and won't let you go to sleep again although it is too late to do anything about it.

You are a visionary and a dreamer and you are likely to have a practical family that keeps a wet blanket handy. Your mother thinks your wife, if you have one, ought to be firmer with you; she even suspects in private that you were better off with her. Your wife lays your peculiarities to your early training and sometimes says to the boy, "You are just like your father." Your mother and your wife are likely to be diametrically opposite types, yet you love both of them and they adore you. Loving and being loved is one of the things you do best of all.

I'VE GOT YOUR NUMBER

You have probably taken at least one correspondence course which you did not finish, entered gymnasium classes which you did not attend, and forgotten important engagements. Nobody knows your faults as well as you do and when you get to heaven you are going to be surprised to see Saint Peter swinging wide the gate and all the lady angels choiring, "Goody, goody, goody, here he comes!"

Key Number 1

VIRTUALLY every woman loves you so much that she wants to start right in making you over. You have a canny streak that enables you to marry one of the few who will love you and let you be as God and your mother made you. The women you do not marry keep right on liking you, and they like your wife too. Sometimes there are so many of these amiable ladies more or less attached to you that they could form a club and call it, "Wives and near-wives of No. One Man."

It is a wonder they are so crazy over you, for you are very, very seldom a good provider. Routine office work is not for you. Too many interesting events are taking place in the world outside. Men of your type do well as reporters, traveling salesmen, publicity and advertising men, and in other jobs that contain a good deal of movement and few long monotonous stretches. Painters, writers, and musicians are very likely to be in this group.

We are not saying that you are lazy, for you are occupied all the time and you would do well in one of the old countries where men are not expected to be everlastingly on the trail of the dollar. You would best express your personality if you had an inherited income and could spend your time traveling (often by air), reading, tinkering around the house, and teaching the children how to make things with their hands. Your tastes are wide; if you raise dahlias, you will find room for pansies also, and you cannot dislike terriers because you enjoy collies. The theater is your hobby.

Key Number 2

OH, HOW fortunate it is that you had a strict bringing up! Because you are the kind of man who is often led into temptation. The fact that you do not yield to it makes you all the more exasperatingly attractive. If you are old enough to have grown up before the days of frank and fearless women, you do not know what dangers you have missed; if you are a modern you have set up a protective mechanism which foils and baffles these same ladies.

You would make a good teacher or social worker, and your ancestors doubtless were ministers. You are a kind person, but you can be cruel without knowing it. You give others fair treatment and expect to be treated fairly yourself. You would be faithful to a job or a wife. You reach your conclusions not by intuition but by hard thinking. You make your best success late in life. Your career is likely to branch away from its original direction. You are very generous but not at all a spendthrift. You are cautious, and though you admire spontaneity in others you suppress it in yourself. You will never lack friends. Your problem is, rather, how to choose from among all the nice people who wish to know you.

You are much more likely to be a writer than an artist, and your writing will be along non-fiction lines. You are so good at anything you undertake that you privately think you could have been an artist, too, if you had wished to be.

You can win just about any woman you want. If you wish people to like you, they have to do it. When you are at your mellow best you cannot be resisted.

Key Number 3

You do not vote the way your father did. In fact, you may not vote the way you yourself did five years ago. You are always hoping that a minority party will be right, because you have no faith in majorities, but you find human nature where you expected pure idealism. As you grow older you are likely to stop voting except in Presidential years, and then you have to become very enthusiastically against one candidate in order to build up your faith in the other. You will never to your dying day learn that ideals are banners waving out of reach of human hands.

You lost your rose-colored glasses young and have never reconciled yourself to their absence. Yet you will try everything once. You have tried love more times than that, and by nature you fall in love gracefully and from experience fall out silently—but black and blue.

Once you almost got into serious trouble when out of the kindness of your heart you tried to save a woman from disaster for which you were in no way responsible; your blood runs cold when you remem-

23

ber what a close shave you had. Since then you have forced yourself to be cold when others have come to you with their lamentations, for experience has taught you that most people get what is coming to them.

If you are a trifle critical of others, you are still more severe on yourself. You underestimate yourself and everybody thinks better of you than you do of yourself.

Key Number 4

PEOPLE get all mixed up about you because you hold tight to your standards, yet never try to impose them on others. The only times your standards cause trouble are when you are linked in business or love with another person whose conduct cannot be reconciled with your code. In such crises you will neither tyrannize nor give in, so there is nothing for it but to separate. Fortunately, you are a good judge of character and seldom become involved in such situations.

You can adjust to other people and to a foreign environment without giving up your own individuality. You can get along very well with people who do not think as you do. But when you choose a wife you want one who is your own kind.

You are domestic and love your home. You have respect for the past and the part your ancestors played in history. Your wife is—or will be—a good housekeeper, as well as entertaining and considerate. She is lucky to have you for a husband and would be the first one to admit it.

25

Key Number 5

WOMEN who are having trouble with their husbands come to you for advice. It's too bad they don't take it. But even if they don't, the good advice you give them makes them all the more fond of you.

You are very considerate of the other person's ego. You will sit through a lecture that bores you rather than hurt the feelings of the lecturer by leaving. Similarly, you might keep on a rather inefficient employee who loved his job, even if you had to do some of his work yourself.

Your appearance is somewhat deceptive. You might pass for a deacon in some church, but at heart you question anything that cannot be proved by chemistry and mathematics. You are very fond of travel, and get a lot out of it. There seems to be some kind of repressive influence in your life, and there are signs of a conflict between your early and present environments. Perhaps you take things to heart more than you need to.

Why not look up some of your old friends? They are wondering why you dropped out of their life.

Key Number 12

NOT all men who come out Number 12 are great, but a surprising number of great men belong in this group. They can succeed in law, music, or publishing. Actors and artists are here, too. The combination of a logical mind with an appreciation of artistic values is what makes them subtle in law or well-balanced in art.

Even the average run of those in this group are greatly helped by having these two sides to their natures. If they do not succeed in business they can at least find something to enjoy when they are unemployed. Life is not boring to them.

To belong to Number 12 indicates foreign influence of some kind. Did you have a Spanish mother? Or is your wife Russian? Or have you lived abroad? You are not more than ninety-nine per cent American.

Key Number 13

MEMBERS of the Anti-Alimony Club almost all belong here. These men are marvelous lovers but erratic husbands—or shall we say spasmodic husbands? Their wives can never be sure of anything about them, not even of their actually preferring the other woman. They are incurable romantics. In every old hag they discern a wilted flower, in every knobby girl a green bud. Virtually all poets belong here; the exceptions are those who write book-length poems.

They suffer intensely and recover. They have to recover. No one could endure such suffering long. Their money-earning ability varies. When they do make money, it goes.

Not only ladies bearing broken hearts follow these men; they are followed by less imaginative men also, who envy the way they make life their oyster.

Key Number 14

YOU may do a lot of things you shouldn't, but you would never be so unkind as to refuse to flirt with a woman who asked for it. Also, you would not go too far. You make an excellent husband because you have a sense of responsibility where women are concerned, as well as a kindly nature.

Don't worry too much if you find it impossible to provide for your women-folk as lavishly as you would like. If you are not making money it probably isn't your fault. You usually consult your wife—if you have one—in business matters.

You are extremely fond of children, and have definite ideas regarding how they should be brought up.

You have a practical streak. If art is your line, it must be applied art. You are more likely to be an engineer.

You do not have to be dragged to parties, you go along quietly. After you get there you have a better time than you expected.

Key Number 15

THERE is something peculiarly lovable about your personality. Every woman knows that she can trust you not to be unkind to her, even if she throws away one of your seventeen pipes. There are plenty of queer, colorful people among your friends. You pride yourself on being able to handle temperamental women. You would be good at taming wild animals.

You look lightly on the faults of those you live with. If they criticize you, you are apt to distract their attention and go on the way you were going. You would rather keep people good-natured than prove your point. You would rather go around an obstacle than over it. You are equally at home in city or country. Or any foreign country, for that matter.

You are likely to marry a bit late, but you will choose a woman of strong personality. She may seem to dominate you, but you will really quietly make her over, until she is everything you wish her to be.

I'VE GOT YOUR NUMBER

You like experiments in food. You can't let the recipe alone; you have to improve on it.

You have a sense of social responsibility, but you refuse to let yourself be bored.

CHARACTER STUDIES FOR MEN

Key Number 23

IF ANYBODY should ask you if you have ever been disappointed in love, you would have to reply, "Yes, always!" Men of Number 23 type are apt to leave behind them a trail of broken engagements, but once married they usually stick it out. They are a trifle cynical about women, because they discover that a girl with a sidelong glance, sleek hair, and a light foot is not necessarily, when married, a clever bridge-player, a good cook, a cheery soul, and a marvel at dressing on no allowance as becomingly as she did when she had her salary. The girl is not likely to be as disappointed in you as you are in her, because she hasn't expected as much.

You get on better in business than in personal relationships, and when you have pulled out of the subordinate positions into leadership you will go far. Subordination is especially difficult for you, because you are not a "yes" man. When you know better than your boss (and you usually are his superior) it is impossible for you to applaud his disastrous policies

37

I'VE GOT YOUR NUMBER

You will do best in a line of work where you are under nobody's thumb.

You have more temptations than most men and are not always successful in resisting them. You are entirely wrong in blaming the tempter when your conscience hurts, because you are really stronger than your associates.

Key Number 24

WHEN you make a mistake you do not hold it against others; you blame nobody but yourself, and say that you have learned your lesson. The mistake is usually not a serious one and you extricate yourself promptly. You do your work well because you like it, and you may have changed professions once or even twice in order to get exactly what suited you. Your chosen work probably brings you in contact with a good many people.

You like to do things for those with whom you deal. In the old days you might well have been a minister, and if you could only feel the call to-day you would be a success in running an institutional church and bringing the men to Sunday services. You would be fine as a lawyer or a doctor or in any position that involves a slightly paternalistic relationship with clients. You would be less successful as a salesman unless you offered something of undoubted value, for you would hesitate to sell a white elephant to an orphan or persuade a widow to buy on the

39

instalment plan. You would try to make even natural-born suckers prudent and thrifty.

Your income is good, though it is never sufficient because you listen to so many calls upon your generosity and collect dependents without trying. You are good to your relatives and give your sisters presents. Your heart is anchored in your home, but sometimes it drags noticeably and your wife is nervous for a time. But you know where you belong and you are contented in your home harbor.

Key Number 25

WHEN you go into the jungle you carry your moral code with you. In other words, though you are an adventurer, you hold on to the principles you learned in your youth. Perhaps, indeed, you turn your moral weapons against the very people who gave them to you. This is the result of having a logical mind. If it were not for your pleasant nature they would not like to have you around the house, but since you have learned to speak the truth considerately they forgive you and ask you to come for another week-end. If a woman wishes to lay her head on your shoulder and tell you her troubles, you feel a bit uneasy. But she finds that you really do wish to help her.

You are very much a part of the modern world and do not hesitate to face any issue squarely or talk with any kind of person or read any kind of book, and yet you never get yourself into trouble.

Key Number 34

THE conflict in your soul is largely due to your thinking that you are not the man you might be. You know all the not-so-admirable acts of your life, and you take it for granted that most other men are snowy lambs—or pale gray at most. You disapprove of a good many things, and the conflict between your ideals and reality makes you unhappy and sometimes irritable. Women can't make you out, but you never give up hoping to find one who will understand you.

Yet how can any one understand you when you are such a puzzle to yourself? Figure out the many different sides to your character and note how they conflict, especially where the ladies are involved. Like Adam, you feel that it wouldn't have been polite to refuse the apple; we hope you do not tell the woman that she shouldn't have offered it.

You suffer from moods of despair during which you are likely to be bitter against those closest to you.

You do your best work when you are part of an organization which is large enough to be impersonal, but which demands the finest that is in each individual. You should combine business and service to the community in your work.

You will be glad—and a little surprised—to hear that many women envy your wife.

Key Number 35

CERTAIN people annoy you very much—for example, well-dressed stoutish ladies leading little dogs, hard-boiled flappers, and business men with a narrow outlook. You think many things that you do not say. We advise you to keep on not saying them.

You would like to write, but you feel that the kind of magazine people buy is not the kind that would take the sort of things you wish to write.

You are very much influenced by the women of your family, but you can resist other women. You are looking for the kind of girl your mother was in her youth, and you have decided that girls of that sort are hard to find.

A cause appeals to you, and you could lead a revolution, but after it was over you would become disgusted with the inefficiency and lack of idealism of the people you had been trying to help. It would be the same old story over again.

You do not go in a gang. Didn't you play by yourself a good deal when you were a child, and room alone at college?

You like the mechanics of radio, but not what comes over the air.

Key Number 45

You can be trusted to help with unemployment relief, and you will even take care of your sister's children in an emergency. You do not pass the buck to other people. Moreover, you are never ostentatious about your good works.

You enjoy a good play or movie better than a wild party. You do not feel entirely at home with the uninhibited. Once in a while you are persuaded against your better judgment to hold opinions that people of your sort do not customarily hold, but when the upsetting influence is removed you are quickly persuaded back again. You feel that you are open-minded at election-time, and will listen to what the other side has to say, but when you go to the polls you vote for the man who stands for doing things in the good old conservative way.

Mature women are your firm friends. You may not get on so well with the immature.

Key Number 123

YOU think that you would get along all right if people would only let you alone. But you don't let them alone. You make them interested in you and of course they hang on your telephone wire and burden the letter-man and drop in when you would like to be alone. Your only hope is a hermit's hut in the wilderness, and you know you will be lonely there. Take women, now. You give them a rush, drop them, and find them still clinging about your neck. Who said woman is like a violet? You find her more of a burdock. Tut, tut, man! Yet it is no use to scold you, for that is the way you are. And Heaven knows you are as disappointed as the woman every time a dream dissolves.

You do better in your work than in your personal relations. The work does not have its feelings hurt when you are annoyed. You can leave it and come back to it. You sometimes say to yourself when women are particularly impossible, "After all, I have my work." If you are not at ease in your profession or business, get some hobby into which you can throw your energy; for you are one who is happier giving himself to a task than receiving favors from others.

Key Number 124

YOU are a good salesman—to use that phrase in its highest sense. You could sell education to impatient young men who long to be out on the football field, health to invalids, homes to families, high-class bonds to widows, and ideals to a soul-sick world. You can do this for two reasons: first because you concern yourself only with those things in which you have complete confidence (and your judgment is excellent), and secondly because of your delightful personality. From the moment you first slewed your infant eyes around to gaze upon your adoring mother, you have had a way with women. Nor did you forget Father in distributing your baby glances. You get along equally well with both sexes.

You can have your own way without interfering with others' comfort. You think there is room for every one in the world and do not try to grab another's place. You have things very much as you wish, and have, too, the approval of those who give in to you.

The chances are you are good-looking. You probably started with a good physique and you do or will steadily overwork yourself. While we hate to tell it to you, your fine spirit shines out through your eyes; but you are not the tiniest bit of a prig. Women fall for you, and you are likely to have difficulty in letting them down easy, without hurting their ego. Your wife (you will have but one) adores you if you are already married; if not, there is competition for the position.

Key Number 125

WATCH that phase in your character which wishes to try experiments. It is a toss-up whether it will lead you to fortune or failure. You finish what you begin, but your danger lies in the possibility that you will hang on to some dear project which would better be abandoned, like a bulldog unable to unlock his jaws from a trouser-leg that had turned out to belong to the policeman instead of to the burglar.

Your type is best off when married to a yielding woman. If you draw one of the kind who wishes her own way there is danger that she will start a nagging campaign or retreat into invalidism in order to express her personality. In that case you will see that she has every comfort and you will spend a good many evenings at the club or whatever gathering-place for men takes the place of a club in your town.

You like to get out into the country, but when you are there it is the city people who are your intimates, although you have plenty of friends among the local people too. When you go to Europe—and how you

53

I'VE GOT YOUR NUMBER

love it!—you wish to see everything, queer little places, mountaintops, and conventional sights. You have virtually no love troubles; if you have, you ought to know what other men go through!

Key Number 134

HOURIS, peris, nymphs, and dryads attend your dreams, but when you awake you find yourself surrounded by wives and mothers and sisters and aunts. Even a sweetheart is only a woman when she comes from the moonlight into the house. How well you know the disillusionment of the morning after and how cynical you get about lipstick and powder. The only woman who never disappoints you is your mother.

You are likely to be widely informed on world topics and to read a great deal. It is probable that you have marked talent in music, writing, or art. A profession involving good taste and clever fingers like draftsmanship or some sort of designing seems more suited to you than auditing or other routine tasks. Money is unimportant to you. You are not very good at earning it, because there are so many interesting things to do which bring in no financial return. You would rather go fishing along a trout stream when the apple-trees are in bloom and the violets dot the banks than clip your own coupons in a stuffy bank

I'VE GOT YOUR NUMBER

vault; particularly if you have to earn the bonds yourself.

It is a question of early environment whether you are more at home on the dance floor or under the cathedral pines of the north woods; whether you sail a catboat in Buzzard's Bay or climb the glaciers of the Canadian Rockies. You were born to be a playboy and only a cruel woman will try to hold your nose to the grindstone; but most women are cruel.

Key Number 135

WHAT are you doing here? Didn't we meet you in Italy or China or South America? How strange that you should pop up in a conventional environment! Perhaps you are still seeking that fine woman destined to be your wife—the woman who will understand you and love you just as you are. Her strength of character is (or will be) a great comfort to you, even though you fight it. And she in return will admire your artistic streak, your originality and your freedom from the small-town standards that restricted her own childhood.

Are you planning to go to Russia? But you would have difficulty in raising the money, and if you did raise it you might prefer Arabia. Anything but a World's Fair.

You tend to be very intimate with people and then somehow lose them in the shuffle, perhaps rediscovering them later. You would love nothing so much as a studio of your own, and you would have a grand time decorating it. If anything could tie you to one spot it would be this.

Key Number 145

How the cat likes to sit in your lap! That is because you understand its personality and consider its feelings. Peace-loving as you are, you will fight the cat's enemies.

You show a streak of small-town and a streak of travel. Perhaps you were born in a small place and then went forth into the world. Wherever you went you made friends. You are cosmopolitan yourself, but very much interested in the man whose horizon is smaller than yours.

As a general rule a man belonging in Number 145 selects his wife wisely. His only danger is that women inclined to be dominating appeal to him. But perhaps he knows what is best for him. Anyway, he gets along well with people, and appreciates the things women do for him, just as they appreciate the many thoughtful, kindly things he does for them. It is so natural to him to be good to women that he is sometimes surprised at their appreciation of acts that seemed to him a matter of course.

Key Number 234

YOU are a repressed Don Juan who might do a lot of harm were it not for the still small voice shrilling like a fire siren in your soul. A hundred years ago you would have worn a parson's high stock and the women of your parish would have gone crazy over you. Here is something for you to think about: you are critical of other people because you are critical of yourself. If you were not so hard on yourself, you would be easier on those about you, members of Congress, and the movie film you saw last night.

Can't you accept the fact of man's imperfection in this mortal state; and woman's likewise? You doubtless think that women should be better than men, and each time an angel proves to be human you have a shock like that of stepping off a step you didn't know was there.

You are good at getting up on time, answering letters promptly, paying bills, denying yourself pleasures you might have, cutting the grass, doing necessary errands, and possibly going to church. But we could forgive you all these excellencies if only you did not so exaggerate your faults in your own mind. We advise tennis, a pup, camping, winter sports, and a lot of dancing, rather than the more sedate recreations like bridge and golf.

Your business future looks good to us, whatever your occupation, because you have the qualities which make for success. If you do not like your line of work, shift to another as soon as the opportunity presents itself; you will always do best in what you like, although you are inclined to force yourself to stick to what you dislike.

Key Number 235

COME, come, don't take the world so seriously. You are upset when the American ambassador dines with the King of England, because of your sympathy with the corner bootblack, who wasn't invited; but you would be just as much upset if the bootblack dined with the king. You champion the oppressed until people stop oppressing them, and then you lose interest in them. The unhappy disturb you because they are not happy, and the happy disturb you because they are not unhappy.

As for women, they disturb you because they are old-fashioned, because they are new-fashioned, because they are gentle and yielding, because they are firm and combative, because they like you and because they don't. But do you give in and give up? No indeed. You set your back against a rock and defy them to come one, come all. You are likely to see your name in the papers and some day you will be either wildly applauded as a leader or sent to jail. Or both.

Key Number 245

YOU do not make friends with women easily; but, your confidence once gained, you are loyal. You are helpless against an aggressive woman, particularly if her predatory nature is hidden behind a helpless manner; once involved with such a woman, you are unable to free yourself.

For a pleasant, rational woman, you make a perfect husband; yes, we said perfect. Your children admire you tremendously as soon as they are old enough to understand you and you are proud of them if they give you the slightest cause for pride; but you are too intelligent to overestimate them. A black sheep in your flock would break your heart, although you would stand by him through thick and thin. You care for more people than you admit.

An administrative position suits you, for you can see the whole as well as the details of a job. You put a lot of yourself into your work. Your pleasures are likely to be something others might consider work, like running a farm on the side or doing carpentry or tinkering with your car, unless you are too tired to do anything but rest. Your honesty rules are well formulated and if you are a lawyer you deal in corporation rather than criminal law.

The worst career you could possibly have would be writing fairy-tales, including romances. You will never be a bigamist nor involved in any money scandal. Neither will you have wild adventures of an emotional or a geographical nature.

Key Number 345

YOU are as complicated as a diagramless cross-word puzzle and as difficult to understand as the new theories of contract bidding. Which of your many personalities is the real you? Your wife—if or when you have one—picks out one side of your nature to love and another to detest. If she is a pleasant woman she talks chiefly about the former and you are a lucky man. You have had the dream of educating a young girl to be exactly the sort of a wife you want, but you have never done it, nor will you, because you would hate to have people laugh at you.

You are pretty good at your work; would rate around ninety-three on a scale of one hundred. You probably stick to one line, although you often consider changing. Day-dreaming is your refuge from harsh realities, but you can always distinguish fantasy from actuality. Many novelists of the older school fall into the 345 class, but few musicians. If you have any leaning toward religion, you would do well in the ministry.

You feel most at home with women older than

yourself or with serious young women, although they have to be easy on the eyes. Do not make the mistake when courting a girl of paying too much attention to her mother, although after you are married it is always pleasant to have your mother-in-law approve of you heartily.

Key Number 1234

YOU are conservative in your behavior but liberal in your thinking. Very possibly you will make a big hit in your work—perhaps in some kind of research. You are likely to marry a gentle, kindly type of woman whom other women like. You will treat her generously, in deeds if not always in words. You have made up your mind, however, not to let any woman get too great a hold on your affections. Let's hope you don't carry out this cold-blooded resolution.

You are stimulating mentally, even though exasperating. No one is ever bored by you. You like discussions that keep you mentally alert. Often you take a side you really do not sympathize with, just to start something. You make an excellent impression on strangers because you have a pleasant, interested manner. If you are married, a good many people come to your house because your wife is the type of woman who attracts company.

Your home is interesting to you. You enjoy doing over the house and adding a new wing to it. The garden, however, is your wife's sphere. This is odd, because usually it is the other way about. You make an excellent father, unless your child is too much like you.

Key Number 1235

YOU are not quite in your normal state, are you? But you are not telling what it is that is eating you. Or have you tried to fool us by answering the questions insincerely? At any rate, there is some conflict here. We have it! You are by nature an explorer, it may be in the scientific laboratory, where you cook in test-tubes, or you may actually have a yen to push into territory where man has never been before. If you started to cross Africa you would not turn back even though you died in the attempt and all your train died with you. Likewise you would arrive at the North Pole even though you left behind you a trail of fingers and toes.

You are not so good as an employer, and not so good as an employee. You do your best work when you are alone. You do not take causes very seriously, although you are willing to argue about them, preferably on the minority side. A temperament like yours is better understood in Europe than in the United States.

Key Number 1245

WHATEVER you do you do well. You know your subject from A to Z and you know how to apply your knowledge. If you are under twenty-five this statement will apply increasingly each year of your life from now on, for you are one who keeps on learning as long as he lives. It is difficult to deduce your profession, because there are so many lines in which you are competent. We can say, however, that it is probably not a solitary occupation, like chemistry, or other forms of scientific research. You are popular in clubs and are always being begged to take the chairmanship of a committee. Invitations are constantly fluttering your way, especially if you are unmarried, but you are careful not to let your social life infringe on your work life.

You can associate with people without serious emotional mix-ups. You have many friends, but few intimates. Perhaps it is because you put so much of your energy into your work or because you spread your liking over so many people, or for both reasons. If you are unmarried, married women are always saying to one another, "Why doesn't he marry?" and inviting you to meet charming girls. It seems to them a slur on womankind that you should be happy unwed.

If you are married, your wife would better be pleasant and reasonable, for if driven too far you are the type to go out and never come back, though you would be polite about it, and continue to support the family. You know where you came from and where you are going.

Key Number 1345

BY NATURE you are a one-life, one-wife man. You would stand a great deal before you would be divorced, but if you are left a widower you will remarry soon. You like to think of yourself as an independent soul, complete and self-contained. Man, it is trying to be what you are not that makes you unhappy. You have a naturally faithful heart hitched up to a wide-ranging imagination—a difficult team to drive. Your business life suffers from the same uneasiness as your emotional life.

You would be good in a long-established business which you could carry on along usual lines, but all the time you would be uneasy because newer firms were branching out in schemes which your experience told you were not sound. In brief, your confidence in yourself is not equal to your ability.

You are critical of the younger generation even while you are yourself one of them. A sense of insecurity has hung over from your childhood. Something kept you from being one of the gang.

75

I'VE GOT YOUR NUMBER

You see more clearly than most people that we are all tight-rope-walkers and that no net is spread beneath to receive us, but since that is life—and death —you will have to develop a philosophical attitude.

Key Number 2345

You can take up a piece of work which some one has promoted and failed to carry on, and disentangle it from its difficulties. You might do this for a bank, a life-insurance company, a welfare organization, or a college. You would not be seriously handicapped by lack of education, for you would educate yourself in the evenings, when other young men were whooping it up. If your first position has vistas you will remain with the same concern all your life. At any rate, you will change only for the better. Your job is likely to stick to you through hard times. Your strength lies in stabilizing rather than in innovating and you are therefore better as an executive than as a promoter.

You are likely to marry late and choose a good wife, who may feel, however, that you are a little hard on the children. You will do much for them, even to the point of making their decisions for them, not realizing that a child's own mistake is better for him than his parent's wisdom.

You dislike people who get away with things, and

I'VE GOT YOUR NUMBER

you are pessimistic about the future—though we think you have no cause to be. Things are likely to turn out very well for you. Remember this prophecy when you have one of those attacks of complete discouragement which frequently beset you.

Key Number 12345

YOU have good concentration, persistence, and accuracy, and because you have these qualities yourself you are apt to be impatient with wool-gatherers, butter-fingers, mistake-makers, and the rest of the common herd. For this reason you are not as good a teacher as you are a doer, and you are miscast as a foreman or a manager.

In a subordinate position you are in danger of having a run-in with the boss, particularly if he is incompetent, as bosses sometimes are. You do your best work in situations where you are responsible for the outcome and are independent of other people. Under such circumstances you will work the clock round, forgetting to eat. This is most annoying to your wife, if you have one, for she thinks that work should be taken in moderation.

You are likely to marry late in life or not marry at all; although that is not the women's fault. The truth is, you can get along without women pretty well; especially can you get on without the emotional turmoil in which they seem to you to live. You are neither a lone wolf nor yet a herd member, but shift from one rôle to the other. This gets you into a lot of trouble, for you will not play bridge when you do not care to, nor are you crazy about charades. You need a hobby and if you have not already provided yourself with one, we suggest canoeing, tennis, hiking, week-end camping, golf, or any other outdoor sport in which you can have company or not according to your mood.

QUESTIONS FOR WOMEN

(Answer the questions yourself; do not let others answer for you.)

GROUP 1

A—Do you tend to choose friends for whom you can do things rather than those who do not need your help?

B—Have you been loved more than most people?

C—Is there something in you that makes it easier for you to give than receive?

D—Should a school-girl tell on another who is cheating?

E—Do you have to guard against a tendency to be wounded by people who do not know they have hurt you?

GROUP 2

A—If a woman brags about her new fur coat, does it serve her right if some one points out that the cut is wrong?

B—Do you take your time when you have at last secured a clerk in a crowded store?

C—Is it fun to take a man away from a girl even if you don't care for him?

D—Do you resent it when your friend makes a hit and you don't?

E—Are you good at getting even with people?

GROUP 3

A—A storekeeper refused to sell a broom to some skaters who wished to sweep snow from ice that he did not consider safe. Would you have refused?

B—Would you refuse to pass the candy to one of your contemporaries forbidden by the doctor to eat sugar?

C—A mother is asked over the telephone to deliver a message to her son who will go back to college the next day. The message is from a reckless young married woman in whom the son is much interested. The mother suspects that it is an assignation. In her place would you suppress the message?

D—Would you refuse to let alcohol be brought into the house if your husband were a heavy drinker?

E—Is it good for freshmen to be kept down?

GROUP 4

A—Do you hope that you, like Peter Pan, will never grow up?

B—Do you sometimes tease a man until he longs to shake you?

C—Are you more likely to be called a kitten than dignified?

D—Are you demure and innocent-eyed when you are putting something over?

E—Were you pretty much indulged as a child?

GROUP 5

A—Are circumstances always upsetting your plans?

B—Have you so many things to think about that you have a sense of confusion?

C—Do you send things back to the stores a good deal?

D—A farmer who had always longed to take a trip went to New York on the money he had saved to reshingle the leaking barn. Could you have done this?

E—A man calling at the Smiths' was told not to take a certain chair because a caster was off. He commented that he had received the same warning when he called a year before. Could this have happened in a house you were running?

KEY NUMBERS FOR WOMEN

0	see page	93
1	" "	95
2	" "	97
3	" "	99
4	" "	101
5	" "	103
12	" "	105
13	" "	107
14	" "	109
15	" "	111
23	" "	113
24	" "	115
25	" "	117
34	" "	119
35	" "	121
45	" "	123

123	see page	125
124	" "	127
125	" "	129
134	" "	131
135	" "	133
145	" "	135
234	" "	137
235	" "	139
245	" "	141
345	" "	143
1234	" "	145
1235	" "	147
1245	" "	149
1345	" "	151
2345	" "	153
12345	" "	155

Key Number 0

WE ADVISE you to make a point of listening at key-holes, because you will hear so many nice things said about you. Even possessive wives and dominating mothers have to admit that you have fewer faults than most.

You are one of the gentle, straightforward, non-aggressive women who take care of themselves in a quiet way. You go directly for what you want, but you do not knife the people who stand in your path. You are tolerant of the opinions of others, yet not easily influenced. Tact and dependability are your long suits.

You like the limelight as well as anybody, but you do not demand it. You do not interrupt. But you can hold up your end of the conversation. You are always interested in what is going on, in the newspapers and out of them.

You do a lot of good, if married, for the family and if unmarried, for the community—possibly for both, if you have the energy. But you will immediately dispute this assertion, for you do not do good

93

I'VE GOT YOUR NUMBER

for the sake of doing good. It is more or less accidental and unintentional. If you have children you are devoted to them.

You are affectionate rather than emotional; consequently your husband will be treated to plenty of companionship and few scenes. You are both introverted and extraverted. You love company, but you also have a certain longing for solitude. You have to rest from people. Probably you have to go off and walk by yourself sometimes. That is what keeps you from a nervous breakdown.

Key Number 1

YOU have a conscientious attitude toward the world in general, yet sometimes remind yourself that, after all, your sphere is your own home and your chief duty is toward your own circle. You would not lead a campaign to get a law changed, but you would contribute toward it. If, however, a member of your family were in distress, you would move mountains before breakfast.

The way you keep house is a credit to your mother, but you let the captain run the ship, whereas your mother probably felt obliged to share this responsibility with her captain, or at least occasionally to go and see whether he was running their ship properly.

You do not practise the usual feminine wiles, and it is often a surprise to other women that the men like you so much when, beyond being pleasant, you seem to be making no effort to attract them.

You would be happy as a spinster, but it would be too bad to deprive some man of such a pleasant, considerate spouse. It is wise for you to marry young,

95

I'VE GOT YOUR NUMBER

because if your parents form the habit of leaning on you they are likely to disapprove of any man who comes courting, and you are not the kind of girl to climb down a rope ladder at night.

Key Number 2

YOU read "The New Yorker," know what's what, who's who, and how to dress. You like the kind of man who dances and dresses well, knows where to go, and how to act when he spills the gravy. Also he must know his onions—especially the kind that grows in the financial district. You are such a good executive yourself that you would be annoyed with a man who tore his coupons instead of cutting them, even though he had plenty of these untidy scraps of paper to heap in your lap.

You stand a little aloof from life, yet know all that is going on. You are not cold-blooded, yet it may be said of you that your heart does not stand in the way of your advancement. You do not have tantrums, nor do you ask for special privileges just because you are a woman. You are a hard worker. You do not baby yourself or anybody else.

You can use your head and think out a problem without being side-tracked by the personal element. You are sophisticated, rather European, in your outlook. You have no desire to be a martyr and do not care to have people look upon you as a poor abused thing. You may not be this age, but you are rather typical of the generation born around 1900.

You can be married any time you wish, or you can live your life serenely without marrying. You are not likely to marry in haste. You look upon marriage almost as you would upon a job. It is something you hope to make good in. If you failed as a wife, your pride would be hurt.

You get a lot of pleasure out of life and comparatively little pain. You long to travel, but would rather not do it till you are able to go comfortably. You are poised, good-humored, and able to take care of yourself. But though you could pay your own way, luckily you do not have to go Dutch treat. The men like to take you places.

You spend plenty on your hats.

Key Number 3

IT IS a curious fact that most of the women of this group are moderns, and about fifty per cent of them wear short hair. They are good at careers, but also very home-loving. A Number 3 woman *will* have a home and a fair amount of physical comfort. They are pretty well dressed, but not models of fashion. They always think that if they had more time or money they'd show people! But as a matter of fact that extra money would go toward installing a furnace.

These women take on the responsibilities that are thrust upon them, but they do not allow themselves to be imposed upon. They are good to their relatives, but likely to live apart from them. They are conscientious about their engagements and on time for their appointments. They usually decline to take on more than they can carry, and will not go on committees unless they are able to do their share of the work. They are emotional about children and have a great sense of responsibility for their welfare. They have a teaching attitude.

A Number 3 woman is apt to get out of the city, and she has a strong feeling that the country must be kept beautiful. Unsightly bill-boards, or tin cans thrown into a country brook, will make her foam at the mouth.

The women of Group 3 can carry on a career even if married, in circumstances that would be too much for most women. They are emotional in other ways than those that concern children, but have a grip on their emotions, and often harness them to their work. They are likely to marry sweet-tempered, devoted husbands who are not long on money-earning but allow their women-folk a lot of leeway. If the husbands are unreasonable the wives are not likely to stand for it.

Key Number 4

THE fact that you make daisy chains does not necessarily mean that you have nothing else on your mind.
If life dealt you a big blow some time back you don't
say much about it—not because you are the kind that
nobly suffers in silence, but because you like to keep
things pleasant. If, in consequence, you do not always
get the credit for the strength of character you possess, you are admired for your good disposition.

You grow very, very fond of people, and it is
harder for you to suppress your affection than to express it. You are almost certain to marry, and you
will be so loyal to your husband that you will feel
perfectly free to flirt with other men while your husband talks on Life in its Larger Aspects, with older
women.

Sometimes there seems to be a barrier between you
and the one you love best; then all at once it isn't
there. You are sensible not to let it worry you. You
may have a career, but managing your family is your
real interest. If you have no children, you are likely
to have a little dog, and nearly slay any one who isn't

kind to it. You dress well and have chic. Probably you are small, but if you are tall you have a dimple— or at least curly hair. You are the type that will be cherished, even in your old age.

Key Number 5

IF YOU feel like it, you put the tomatoes in a green bowl on the dining-room table because they are beautiful. You do not think it matters much if dinner is half an hour late, but you do think it is important to keep people from disturbing your husband when he is working. You would love to spend a year abroad, and would get more out of it than most people. Perhaps you have already managed it. You have considered art as a career, but probably have not gone very far with it. You do not belong to the conventional set of people your age. More unusual people please you better.

It is a standing joke that you are late for appointments. Nevertheless your friends keep on making engagements with you, taking your failing into account. They remember that you are always good-natured about other people's failings. There is nothing of the policeman in you. Nor is jealousy your weakness. You can admire the work of people who surpass you even in your own line. Your friends are always saying that if you would only exert yourself you could be famous.

I'VE GOT YOUR NUMBER

But you are not naturally aggressive. Your tempo is slow, and you are likely to find yourself married to a man of high-strung, tense nature, whom you will try very hard to please.

Key Number 12

THE influences of your childhood tended to make you close up, rather than expand. Were you not the queer child on the block, and perhaps a bit proud of it? Being an adult pleases you better than being a child, because you have new outlets. But even so, you keep, secretly, a dissatisfied feeling. You are not adjusted to a free-for-all fight now any more than you were as a child. Competing is not in your line. You want honor and position, but you do not go after them aggressively.

This does not mean that you shirk adult responsibilities. Indeed, you accept them prematurely, and the person you can't stand is the fluffy cutie who shirks her share of the work and is admired for it. As for an irresponsible man—well, he'd better keep out of your way.

If you will give up your time-wasting antagonisms you will be a splendid person. You have an excellent head and capable hands. Be the affectionate person you were meant to be instead of the person embittered by undeserved unhappiness.

Key Number 13

THIRTEEN in this case is a lucky number. Women of this group are the salt of the earth, and they have not lost their savor. As teachers, doctors, writers, or office workers they win recognition, but often they are also excellent mothers, bringing up children who are a credit to their parents.

Women of the group are extremely fond of children, and often work with them when they have none of their own. They can forgive a lot more in children than they can in adults. Kindergarten specialists, experimenters in education, children's doctors, and Montessori mothers are to be found here. In other words, they are all-round successful women, much respected by their friends and neighbors. They make good ministers' wives or pioneers, but they are not always so good at being mothers-in-law unless they have previously prepared themselves for the inevitable.

Their pet aversion is the woman who palavers. An insincere compliment irritates them. Instead of taking praise lightly they are apt to ask themselves if they deserve it, and if they decide that they don't they feel almost insulted. After this, let them calm themselves with the thought that probably they do deserve all the compliments they get. Any one who wants to say something pleasant to them can easily find something that is also true.

Key Number 14

THERE'S not a chance for you to die a spinster unless you are shipwrecked on a desert island. You have plenty of partners at dances, because your feet are nimble, your frock becoming, and your disposition good. You can take care of yourself without being a prig, and nobody says things behind your back that they wouldn't say to you.

If you are married your mother-in-law likes you. Your husband thinks you are adorable even if he sometimes threatens to choke you. When he kisses you good-by you give your attention to the rite and do not murmur absent-mindedly, "Don't forget to pay that coal bill to-day"—although you do a good deal of worrying in a strictly private way. You do not boss your children, but you let them know what's what, and after that you expect them to accept the responsibility for their conduct. You are not one to keep them babies forever.

When you meet an old school friend she always talks about how adorable you were in school, and the various members of your family still tell stories about the charming things you did as a little girl.

Key Number 15

DO NOT start that tea-shop, for you will give away so many free meals to your friends that you will fall behind in the rent, and that will bother you, for you are very conscientious.

Here is another example of the way your conscience works: You make casual promises and then feel obliged to keep them, even though it turns out to be very inconvenient.

People have a way of imposing on you. But you are not resentful, even though you feel you have cause to be. You do not dwell on your grievances. You get over a disappointment, and are ready to start something new.

You are not good at letter-writing. You would rather telephone—and the telephone company prospers from your long-distance calls. You are very popular. Your adult relatives may criticize you, but your children will adore you and will side with you against any one. You are likely to have a good many children, and ninety-nine out of one hundred of them will turn out well.

Key Number 23

How you hate a dumb Dora, or a butter-fingers, or any other stupid female creature! You are kinder to clumsy men, perhaps because of the admiration that gleams in their eyes—for men always do admire you, even when they are afraid of you.

You are, yourself, as smart as a whip; and sometimes as biting; though we must allow that the hurts you deal are usually unintentional. You are so accustomed to facing the bitter as well as the pleasant truth about yourself that you do not realize how tender-minded creatures shrink. You tend to cover your emotion with sharp speeches. We wonder why. Is it possible that you too shrink from the truth when it reveals you in your gentler aspects?

You make a good executive, and your subordinates work well for you, valuing your least word of praise. If you have an inefficient boss you do most of his or her work in addition to your own. Business offices are full of unknown secretaries like yourself upon whom the limelight never shines, while the officials get the credit.

I'VE GOT YOUR NUMBER

You are a marvelous housekeeper, whether you do your own work or direct a staff of servants. Your husband is proud of you when you give a party or when he takes you anywhere.

Women of Type 23 tend to marry, and marry well. They choose efficient men, and if these men lack ambition their wives supply it. They choose unusual friends because they can't stand being bored. Their daughters are often more up-and-coming than their sons, but their sons adore them.

Key Number 24

HERE we have the original of the little girl who had a little curl! Nearly all the time she is very, very nice, but once a week she is horrid. Yes, young lady, horrid. A person with your sense ought to know better. The men are more ready to forgive you than the women, partly because you are more careful how you handle them. You really like men better than women, and the painters and plumbers who work for you sing your praises. Yet at that, a woman who deserves your admiration will get it. Men get it often whether they deserve it or not.

You are ambitious and likely to succeed. Your husband probably will be a money-maker. But you are a good sport, and will not reproach him if he goes through hard times. This is one reason why you will hold him. Another is that you are nearly always amusing. You'll laugh at or with yourself or anybody else.

You are a good housekeeper and do things when they ought to be done. You are also a good fighter when necessary. You are not the kind to sit quietly back and let some other woman do the campaigning while you get the benefit of her campaign and at the same time preserve your reputation for sweetness.

Key Number 25

YOU do not receive much encouragement in your plans, and it is hard for you to go ahead without it. People do not like to see you undertake things that may prove to be beyond your strength.

You do not take people at their face-value and will not pretend to. But you are equally ruthless with yourself. In fact, you like to make yourself out worse than you really are. You wish to avoid the pain that comes from disillusionment, so you give yourself a chance to be pleasantly disappointed, rather than unpleasantly. Perhaps you met with disillusionment early in life.

You are by no means a reformer type. It is part of your creed to let others alone and not try to change them. Earnest women who go about doing good are very amusing to you. So are the ones that fuss over curtains and work themselves to death decorating the cake with curlicues.

You would rather talk with interesting men who have achieved things than go to a lively party. A book often means more to you than a visitor. You are not particularly at home with children; in fact, the older people are the better you like them. You work hard at anything you undertake. When you grow tired you become discouraged and wonder if life is worth living. Fortunately, you decide that it is, though you are not over-enthusiastic about it. Art in some form really means something to you—almost more than people. Probably music is your hobby.

When you answered the questions, you were more truthful than you thought. Also we heard you say that we were not to sugar-coat your pill.

Key Number 34

YOU have a way with you, madame—or mademoiselle—Number 34, and if you are unmarried now, you won't be much longer. Men just naturally marry you and you couldn't make them stop even if you wished to. It is especially necessary for you to decide carefully which man you shall allow the privilege of being your husband, for you are the sort who gives her affection once for all. Unless something very unusual happens you will be like the heroine of the old-fashioned love-story who goes to the altar in a haze of bliss and lives happily ever after.

You throw yourself into affairs that interest you, with an energy that is often beyond your true strength and makes other women say, "I don't see how she does it!" If you have to do housework, you make no fuss about it, though probably your main interests lie elsewhere.

You love children and animals and are good at bringing them up; if there is a flaw in your method, it is that you do not throw them enough on their own resources, but tend to give them too much attention.

If you are a salary-earner, you work best in co-operation with other people. You do your share and more, but you see that no one else shirks.

Key Number 35

YOUR consideration for other people gets in the way of your advancement—and the consequence is that everybody loves you. So you're much happier in your smallish circle than you would be if you tried to be famous. There is nothing in the world you will not do for those you love, and it is extraordinary how successfully you love difficult cases. It is almost a pity if your husband is easy to live with, because you can be happy with the sort of men whose wives write letters to the advice columns.

You love cats, and let them impose on you. You cannot be angry with them no matter what they do, but oh! how furious you are with some one who ill-uses them!

You have a great sense of responsibility, not only for the cats that people going away cruelly leave behind, but also for human beings turned astray. You are generous, and are always giving unexpected little presents.

You are by no means a door-mat. You will not let yourself be imposed upon by a friend, a relative, or a husband—indeed, by anything less than a cat. You give an impression of strength and placidity. If the main course burns when you have company for dinner, you can serve the rest with easy grace.

One last secret. Forgive us for telling it out loud, but you have a kind, kind heart.

Key Number 45

How you do love color! New clothes are plumage to
to you and satisfy your artistic sense. It is to be hoped
that your husband will stop reading the newspaper
long enough to admire the new gown and the hat
that sets it off so perfectly. You will have to forgive
him if he is a bit casual about it, for you married—
or will marry—a practical man.

More than likely you are called by a diminutive of
your real name, but if your daughter is named for
you she probably will use the name in full for herself.
People will sometimes say you seem more like sisters
than mother and daughter.

You are inclined to be sensitive, aren't you? But
you take such an interest in life that you soon forget
your hurts. You are always ready for a good time.
One side or other of the arts appeals to you strongly.
Probably you are very fond of music. You are not
too fond of housework. You would rather arrange a
color scheme for the dining-room table than prepare
the meal.

People are always glad to see you coming, because

you take a kindly interest in them and have plenty of news to tell them. You are friendly and get acquainted easily. A new friend is exciting to you, but there is plenty of room in your heart for the old ones too.

Key Number 123

IF YOU were bedridden in an upstairs chamber you would still order the meals and decide when the pantry floor was to be washed, for you are a capable manager and have accepted the responsibilities that go with managing. You are good in executive work, and enthusiastic about any new job, but after a while you become disgusted with the inefficiency of your associates.

You are at your best in crises. You set your infant-in-arms on the bank by the roadside while you change the tire yourself. You have great powers of endurance. Crossing the plains in a covered wagon would have been pie to you. Perhaps one of your ancestors did it.

You can make a funny story out of anything—especially about people. You can keep a straight face when they make absurd remarks or do naïve things, but later, when you are in the bosom of your family, your amusement has to come out.

If you have children you take them seriously. You are so careful of them that you build a little fence around the family. The danger is that you are so efficient that you may take the hammer away from your daughter—or even your husband. But the chances are that you are keen enough to realize this danger.

One strange thing about the 123 group is that it includes both radicals and conservatives. You may be writing articles for the liberal magazines, or you may be working to bring people back to the Church.

Key Number 124

YOU are often called a clever little thing, but you are even more clever than people think. If men realized how keen you are they would be afraid of you, instead of buzzing around you like bees around a columbine. It takes a woman to see how you get away with murder. Sometimes your husband suspects, but when that thoughtful, bewildered look comes into his eyes you are quick to snuggle into the crook of his arm and rub the worry lines off his brow. You're a crooner by instinct, and you know that a tired man relaxes to a lullaby like a sleepy baby.

You are not by a long shot the "saint on earth" that men think you, but neither are you "that demon" a jealous woman once called you. It is lucky for other women that you have a hard-working conscience, for that alone keeps you out of alienation suits and the tabloids. Women of Group 124 are likely to have bachelor sons, while their daughters, like their mothers, marry young.

Key Number 125

PRETTY nearly every unhappiness that could come to you has arrived on time, and you expect the rest of them rather soon. Perhaps the explanation is that you are so much more sensitive than the average person that you suffer more from the bumps of life. This same ultra-sensitiveness will, unless you are careful, make you envious of those tough-minded individuals who grab the gay of life and let the sadness go.

You have a tendency to brood, it is hard for you to forget, and you are constantly disappointed in your expectations. Nobody knows this but you, because you don't talk about it; on the contrary, you are noted for your cheeriness and bravery. You have given up many trips and other pleasures for the sake of those who do not always appreciate your quiet sacrifices.

Key Number 134

WHEN you go down the street you have a cheery word for every one. You are popular with the tradespeople, but all the same they have found that they must give you good service. Your husband adores you. He is inclined to tell every one how wonderful you are, and he loves to give you new clothes and the good-looking shoes that are your specialty. You look your best in pale blues or soft rose.

You would rather have a small circle of friends who understand and sympathize than a crowd of casual acquaintances. You would rather be adored by a few than popular with many. Your intimates appreciate your attitude toward life and the almost oldfashioned stress you put on moral values. You definitely try to keep trivialities in their proper place, for you know that they are the weeds in your garden and must not be allowed to choke the real flowers.

You are likely to marry a man who is at once protective and liberal. He will be ready to take care of you, but he will let you have your say when something has to be decided. You gain your main object my yielding in minor matters.

Key Number 135

THE women of this group are the women who make up the welfare organizations and carry on church work; they are apt, in fact, to take on more activities than they have time or strength for. Are not most of the following things true of you? Your telephone is constantly ringing. Your desk is piled with unanswered letters. You always pay your bills, but sometimes you lose them. You are more critical of yourself than of other people. If you are married, you are a devoted wife and know a good deal about your husband's business life. You would not keep your child from going out to play just because there was a hole in his stocking. You know about your charwoman's troubles and give her advice which she never follows and sympathy which she laps up. Your conscience makes you assume more responsibility than one woman can carry.

Your heart reaches out to gather in from among your relatives, church acquaintances, and business colleagues a group of intimates whom you love and worry about. You speak to the children you meet in the streets and you receive a large number of Christmas cards.

CHARACTER STUDIES FOR WOMEN

Key Number 145

YOU are sensitive to criticism but not resentful of it. You will not fight the person who opposes what you wish to do, but your spirits will droop and you will lose interest in your plan. Then suddenly something will happen that will show you how fond people are of you and how much you are needed, and your spirits will revive like a garden after a shower.

You are considerably disturbed by the trouble the world gets itself into, but you don't know what you are going to do about it. Finally you decide that you will simply do what good deeds you can and hope that the naughty world will be brightened by them.

You are more likely to drift into marriage than to go after it. Women of Group 145 are those lucky sisters who are the selected rather than the choosers. Don't marry a man who threatens to commit suicide. Let him throw himself into the river at once, because if you marry him he will never forget that you yielded to whimpering. You have a better chance with a tyrant, for you will not resent his egotism and that will make him feel kindly toward you. If you are an invalid he will take good care of you.

I'VE GOT YOUR NUMBER

You are indeed the ideal wife for a great big brute of a man. As a widow you are irresistible. Home rather than an office is your sphere. You have difficulty opening windows that stick, remembering what you need at the grocer's, or getting work out of servants, but you are simply grand at admiring the people who come to your assistance. Now, one difference between a woman and a man is that a woman gets bored helping another woman, while a man falls in love with her.

We can't believe that you are not already married. Oh, engaged! You'll make a sweet bride.

Key Number 234

FOR an artistic person you are surprisingly practical. If your literary efforts succeed you'll get your royalties all right. Temperament you have, but you know when to keep it under.

You have sympathy, too, but you do not let it run away with you. You tend to see the Japanese point of view when there is trouble in the Orient, and sometimes you stand up for Mussolini. People are always surprised at that. The secret is that while you are very sympathetic toward the oppressed, and make a point of giving money to street singers, you identify even more with the person who wants something very badly and goes after it.

Things never came to *you* because you sang and held out a cup. You had to work for your success. There was at least one dependent person in your immediate environment who stood between you and the life you wanted, and your problem was to get to your goal without harming that person. You are already on your way.

You are one who knows the lure of the theater.

Key Number 235

LET your motto be, "Be good, sweet maid, and let who will be clever," because for you cleverness is the most natural thing in the world, while goodness does not cloy your life. We do not mean that you commit the sort of crimes that send one to prison; your acts may even accord with the Ten Commandments, but oh, what wives do say of you when their husbands praise you!

We think that the trouble lies right here: You are more discerning than most men and women and instead of accepting the faults you discover in them, and making allowances for those to whom the fairy godmothers gave beauty instead of intelligence, or riches instead of common sense, you are outraged by their dumbness. You are better with dogs and horses because you do not expect them to climb trees when they were not made for that sport.

You must work out a better social technique. You are not happy inside the wall you have built about yourself, so start right in taking it down brick by brick. Remember that if a person hasn't one fault, he usually has another. Say to yourself, "I will love a little to-day and a little more to-morrow and a whole lot on Wednesday." Bigger and better loving. Begin with mass loving and work it down to one selected object.

Key Number 245

LIFE tends to put you in a place that does not satisfy you, but when those who are fond of you try to change things for you, somehow the result is not what you want, either. You always have an unsettled feeling, as if you were wasting your time. Sometimes you take up causes—the kind that people disapprove of— but you drop them before long.

Your feeling of unrest may be a hang-over from an unsettled childhood. You may have had parents who went in different directions. You have never reconciled yourself to life as it is, because your imagination is vivid enough to show it to you as it might be. When the "might be" becomes "is," it isn't the way you pictured it. You are likely to smoke continuously in the hope that it will ease your nerves.

Whether you marry or not depends on chance, for you are not one who bends fate to her wishes. You were Father's girl when you were a tot, and this makes you a man's woman, and you find women catty, though you deny this if your technique is good.

I'VE GOT YOUR NUMBER

If and when you are married you never try to run your husband's business, nor do you rush out to make a career of your own. If you are not married and working you change jobs frequently.

Key Number 345

THERE are not many people of this type. It must be that you had parents who were very different from each other, and you inherited certain traits from one and almost contradictory traits from the other. The result is that one side of your nature won't put through what the other side has decided upon. Trouble sometimes results. You find that you have undertaken to do things that you are not willing to finish. Also you find yourself in a position that you cannot explain with any consistency.

For example, you might make a man give up some really important engagement in order to be on time for the show he is going to take you to, and then be late for it yourself. It's a mercy you have the kind of smile that makes people forgive you. Or if you lived in the country and your cow strayed, you would have the whole neighborhood chasing it and then neglect to head it off when it was passing your own gate.

You are not so good at driving a car, yourself, but when some one else is driving you are eager to tell him how. But the situation is relieved by the fact that you know quite well that your position is untenable, and it's all a joke anyhow. The kind of men who like you are those who are escaping from a Puritanical bringing up.

Key Number 1234

YOU have a sense of the dramatic, and if you are not on the stage you find your drama in everyday life. You would enjoy having your husband fight the man who insulted you, even more than you would enjoy the insult. You realize the importance of clothes and enjoy wearing an unusual combination of colors.

You make a point of being nice to old ladies and remember to send birthday cards to people others forget. If you have no children you have pets if it is possible, and you like odd creatures, like monkeys.

If necessary you can support yourself, and if you are the head of the house you make money go a long way. You are conscientious in both your social relations and your work.

The men who write songs like "A Flower from My Angel Mother's Grave" and "Down by the Window where my Mother Used to Pray" are sons of women of Group 1234. Husbands of these women chorus, "Woman is a mystery." This is partly because you often use indirect methods to achieve your aim in-

stead of steam-roller opposition. What a foreign dip-
lomat you would have made! Your skill in finesse
would be a dangerous weapon in the hands of a less
conscientious woman, but you use it for good.

Key Number 1235

YOU are out of sympathy with this generation. All the things you hold dear they ridicule; the things that seem glamorous to them look tawdry to you.

You live your life for others, but don't get much out of it. Sometimes it seems to you as if you would actually go mad if those for whom you are responsible keep on going against your advice. You could truthfully say (as you sometimes do, we fear!), "I told you so!" You cannot always resist commenting, "If you had followed my advice you would never have got in this jam." It seems to you as if they were possessed to do exactly the opposite of what you wish.

The fact is that you are butting your head against the stone wall of human obstinacy, and you hurt yourself. Why not leave the stone wall alone? Accept the situation and let people go the wrong way. Why should you always try to save them from their just deserts?

Key Number 1245

WHILE you dream of the big things you would like to do, you get a great deal of pleasure out of little things—the luncheon party, the prize pansy from your garden, and the little dog barking at a squirrel.

You are not so dissatisfied with life as you may think. Although it is true that circumstances keep you from doing what you wish to do, it is also true that you would have an uneasy feeling if you could no longer blame circumstances for your inaction. You would feel as if your bluff had been called.

You get great pleasure out of reading and like to write people about the books you read. There is a woman in your family who is something of a problem to you. You feel that she will not accept your advice and at the same time tries to dominate you. Sometimes you resist; sometimes you yield. But you do not resent the domination of a man; in fact, you rather like it.

Key Number 1345

YOU work your best for other people. You could never put the effort into your own advancement that you put into doing things for others. The unfortunate part of the situation is that after you have given your best to some one (probably some one who writes, plays, or paints) you feel a certain proprietary interest in that person. You are a mother to him, and even if you do not care to marry him yourself you wish to pick out his wife for him.

You have high ideals, definite standards of what is right and what isn't, and great powers of endurance. You are not entirely in sympathy with the modern world. You feel that people "get away" with too much.

You will never desert a relative in her old age. You feel responsible for the welfare of those even distantly related to you. Also a stray kitten is your problem. You may solve it by taking it in, even if you have six little kittens already.

Guard against over-possessiveness, leading to jealousy without foundation. The only possible way you can lose your loved ones is by smothering them in affection.

Key Number 2345

THIS lady will make her presence felt in the world. They will always have some new story to tell about her. Her male relatives will be constantly flying to her rescue when she gets into scrapes. Fortunately, she is likely to marry young, so that the responsibility for getting her out of the hands of outraged authority will be divided.

Without understanding much about the value of money, she will get hold of plenty of it. But there will be interim periods when she will be on the rocks. Or in Reno.

She has a good head, but not the kind that will get her far in college. She can drive a motor-car, but it will be well to draw up at the side of the road when you see her coming. Many a man will fall in love with Miss 2345 and talk about her, in his old age, to the more domestic woman on the other side of the hearth.

Key Number 12345

YOU sometimes quarrel with your relatives, but in your heart you know that they are your best friends. You are loyal to childhood associations, and the ties of blood are strong in you.

You give more than you receive, partly because you have a better giving than receiving technique. You are likely to make a joke when you say thank you. Sometimes even a joke about the present.

You do not wish any one to feel sorry for you, and you are resentful of sympathy even when you want it and deserve it. There is a crust over your real self, and you pride yourself on showing the worst side to people. You are wrong in this. Let your fun-loving side come out, and accept the opportunities that come to you for a good time.

You know how to get fun out of life. Even little things like the comic supplements amuse you. You like children and love to give them presents. But they can get on your nerves, too. Dogs and cats come to you and love you because you do not shut them out of your heart as you do people. There is no barrier between you and animals; you are your real self with them.

Life has many pleasures in store for you. Watch for them.

(6)